ABSOLUTE DISASTER!

ABSOLUTE DISASTER!

A VERY BRITISH GUIDE TO THE CINEMATIC APOCALYPSE

Written and illustrated by

TOM J BARROW

CONTENTS

FOREWORD

 take one last deep breath as I slowly dip my head beneath the surface.

The water trickles through my hair, as the last remaining strands slowly turn wet. My ears become muffled by all the strange underwater echoes around me.

I wipe the last remaining drips of condensation from around my goggles as I slowly look around my new submerged surroundings.

"Duunnn dunnn..."

I try to focus what's ahead of me as I swim down into the murky depths. I stare endlessly through the cloudy soup…Then I see it!

Lying in front of me is a huge metal grate. The pressure increases around my ears as I swim further towards it. I coyly reach out with my left hand and reluctantly rasp the metal structure with my knuckles. It eerily echoes throughout the water.

"Duuunnnnnnnn dun.."

My puffy cheeks soon start to wobble as the air behind them slowly dissipates. Before returning to the surface, I need to figure out just what this is. Is it a gateway? A barrier keeping us in? Or…is it keeping something out?

My mind instantly wanders to the absolute worst thing I can think of. A sense of overwhelming dread suddenly overcomes me.

"Duuunnnnnnnnn dun.."

Sh-Sh-Shark!

I start to panic as the last remaining dregs of air disappear from my blood stream. I need to get to safety. Quick!

"Dun Dun Dun Dun Dun Dun Dun Dun Dun Dunnn dunn Dun Dun Dunn Dunnnn"

SWIM YOU FOOL, SWIM!

I erupt through the surface like a Russian Nuclear Sub and inhale a huge gasp of air. All I can hear is the London Symphony Orchestra playing the *Jaws* theme directly into my brain!

"Durh-nerrr-nerrr! Dunnn-dun durrrrh dunnn der-dunn-dun-neer!"

I wildly thrash my legs as they violently splash water everywhere. IT'S RIGHT BEHIND ME!

"DUN-DUN-DUN-DUN-DUN-DUN-DUN-DUN-DUUUN-DUNNN!"

Suddenly my hand slaps against a wall as both knees painfully whack against the side. I quickly clamber to get both of my legs out intact.

Ignoring the pain, I launch myself out of the water and land in a breathless pile at the side. I made it! The shark didn't get me!

Exhausted, I lie on my back against the cold, slippery ceramic titles. I then catch my breath as I stare upwards and slowly close my eyes.

"Phwwwwweeeeeeehht!"

An almighty ear-piercing whistle suddenly breaks the silence.

The ten-year-old me swiftly sits up and looks across the deep-end of my local swimming pool. I see a rather annoyed young lifeguard with a whistle. He angrily points at me, then slaps a metal sign saying, "No Splashing!"

I sheepishly get up and walk away. Didn't he know I was mere inches away from being eaten alive by a giant shark?!

Overactive imagination

Looking back now, it's ridiculous to even think how a great white shark could have ended up in a swimming pool in the middle of land-locked Cheshire!

The mysterious grate; all part of the pool's pump system. Not the gateway to some elaborate grand shark tunnel stretching all the way to the River Mersey!

I've always had an overactive imagination, fueled in part by the fear of the unknown, getting hurt…or worse, being eaten alive! Growing up in the '80s and '90s, the world of film and television were my mirror to the rather traumatic world outside.

As a kid, I was scared of everything:

Darth Vader, Stormtroopers, the IRA, sparklers, "those hooded demon things" in Ghost (1990), salmonella, getting bitten while on the toilet by a snake, Freddy Krueger, vampires, Cybermen, McDonald's Hamburglar, thermo-nuclear war and the Honey Monster.

Thanks to *Jaws*, sharks were my number one source of childhood trauma. To this day I won't go swimming in the sea. It could be Blackpool or Barbados, either way I still refuse to get my feet wet!

The BBC appeal programme *Crimewatch* in particular was horrifying, its factual reconstructions were pure nightmare fuel. Many episodes featured balaclava-garbed men peering through people's kitchen windows in the dead of night!

"Don't have nightmares, do sleep well"- Yeah right, that's easy for you to say!

As I turned older though, like everyone else, I learned to rationalise my fears, and my imagination was drastically tamed. Gone were all those random thoughts of bad guys out to get me.

I was never really in any danger of finding a shark at the bottom of a swimming pool. And as for the Honey Monster, well, all he could threaten me with nowadays is diabetes!

However, when I was sixteen, in the summer of 1998, one film caught my attention. Its nightmarish visions have forever been burnt into my memory ever since. It's not the type of film you're expecting.

There's no scary monster or masked psycho in sight. This was an altogether different kind of horror!

Surf's up!

The film was *Deep Impact (1998)*, a slightly restrained science fiction film starring Morgan Freeman, Elijah Wood and Téa Leoni. The film plots humanity's final days as a comet approaches on a direct collision course to destroy the Earth.

It's a pretty unassuming and melodramatic film, where most of the exciting stuff happens at the very end. The film kicks into gear during the last 20 minutes, when a piece of the comet (1.5 miles wide) ploughs into the US Atlantic coast.

What proceeds is a horrifying chain of events, when a huge thousand-foot-high tsunami smashes into the US east coast, destroying major cities including New York City, Boston and Washington DC.

The wave heads 650 miles inland, destroying countless cities and towns along the way. Granted, in the last twenty-two years, the special effects have aged really badly. My mum's old Nokia phone has a better graphics card in comparison!

Despite the ropey pixels, there's no denying the terrifying thought of your entire world coming to an abrupt end under the shadow of a monstrous wave. On-screen, the tsunami's speed, power, and ferocity is essentially the natural world's equivalent of a nuclear bomb.

It's the ultimate destroyer and leveller of worlds. It would be horrifying to see something as powerful as the ocean suddenly rise up and destroy everything in its path, especially if you lived hundreds of miles away from the coast.

There's no depiction of the wider world in peril, as all the on-screen destruction takes place from a US perspective only. However, towards the end there is a glimpse of the fate of the rest of the world. On-screen, President Beck (Morgan Freeman) gives a speech in front of a partially rebuilt Capitol Building.

Here he states, *"the water's receded"*, but he also adds that *"the wave struck the coasts of Africa and Europe too"*.

As this destruction happens across the other side of the world off-screen, it's stuck with me, wondering how the UK would really fare in this situation. Would we be hit badly? Could the wave reach my hometown of Northwich? Would I at least get my feet wet?

The scene I find particularly disturbing is when the wall of water approaches a small rural community. It's beyond chilling, especially considering how far the wave must have travelled inland. It's equally disturbing when you think you're never more than 70 miles from the sea at any one time in the UK. Gulp!

The paranoia could have got the best of me. Imaginary sharks were nothing in comparison. With so many unanswered questions, I went searching the internet.

Despite a questionable browser history, I didn't get any of the answers I was looking for, and so I was left to ponder the 'what if' questions left by the film for many years to come.

2020

2020 was a year many of us would like to forget. The world was faced with an all too real global catastrophe of its own. As the COVID-19 pandemic ravaged communities, brave emergency workers and care staff rallied around the sick and rushed to save lives.

I'd like to think I did my bit. Yet all I was required to do was sit on my bum all day and watch *Homes Under the Hammer* in my pyjamas. Like so many others, I was furloughed and ordered to stay at home. It was a strange and challenging time.

Like most, I felt powerless and guilt-ridden, especially under the light of the never-ending depressing news coverage.

I count my blessings I wasn't personally affected by the pandemic, but for many, it was a truly horrific time. Thank god for all those FaceTime and Zoom calls with my parents' foreheads. You'd have to laugh to keep from crying.

Above all I desperately wanted to get away from all the misery and endless purgatory of lockdown isolation. And so, I began to hatch an escape plan – well, in my mind that is.

Taking out my DVD collection, I revisited some of my favourite films. I even watched old disaster films, just to make me feel better about the real-life turmoil unfolding around me. My logic was that this world was depressing, but at least we weren't being taken over by aliens or enduring giant tsunamis.

Then it struck me. I remembered my unanswered questions from a few years back; what if something far worse happened to the UK? Not just in *Deep Impact*, but for a host of other films too.

What if we faced the absolute worst of the worst that these films offered? Could we survive? Or would we all need to buy extra toilet rolls and take out home contents insurance?

With my work laptop slowly gathering dust upstairs and a lot of spare time ahead of me, this was my opportunity to start a project and delve deep into the world of apocalyptic cinema.

Risk factor

The aim of *'Absolute Disaster'* is simple: to take one film at a time and imagine what would happen to life in the UK beyond the silver screen. This book will take a uniquely British perspective on how we'd all survive and cope throughout some of cinema's craziest disasters.

Its aim is to fill in the blanks left by some of the biggest blockbusters and explore the theories, logic and reasoning behind them.

The ten chosen films all capture a range of genres and subjects stretching over twenty years from 1995-2015. They've been selected because they all genuinely pose a risk to life across the UK, on-screen and beyond.

The book is split into four categories. The first section, **Terror Technology**, covers a group of films in which our reckless obsession with technology inevitably pushes humanity to the edge of the precipice.

And if humanity wasn't bad enough at destroying itself, **Alien Invasion** looks at what happens when extra-terrestrials travel billions of light-years to come and have a pop at us!

Nature Strikes Back! meanwhile intends to play into our Great British preoccupation with the weather and looks at what happens when Mother Nature has finally had enough of the lot of us.

Finally, **Brave New Worlds** looks towards the future, where humanity is plunged into several post-apocalyptic wastelands. It's mullets and leather chaps from here on in, I'm afraid!

Whilst most of the films in this book stay purely in the realms of fantasy, some will most definitely surprise you, as they unexpectedly veer towards the 'central reservation of reality', more than you might have expected.

Rules

The risk factor and approach to the book is based on a set list of rules and criteria:

1. Each film must have a series of chronological events based on locations that can be followed on or off the screen. Logical predictions and assumptions can then be based on these facts.

    For example, I love Tim Burton's schlock alien invasion classic, *Mars Attacks* (1996). However, there is no clear structure to the invasion so it wouldn't be considered.

    In essence, *Mars Attacks* is a series of visual gags featuring random global monuments being blown up. All we can assume is there might be some kind of 'Stonehenge Jenga', but apart from that it would be difficult to work out.

2. The second rule is: 'the world must go on'! Any film where the whole world ends or is set to end would make a very short chapter indeed.

    So, films like *Armageddon* (1998), *The Hitchhikers Guide to the Galaxy* (2005) and Nicolas Cage's *Knowing* (2009) aren't included.

3. Each chapter is based purely on cannon material. All the events featured are only referenced from watching the films on their own.

   Prequels and sequels are referenced, however any expanded universe material including books, comics and TV series are ignored.

4. The book is not endorsed by any film director, producer or studio. Instead, it intends to act as an irreverent viewer's guide to each film, also exploring the possibilities beyond the screen.

   Each chapter is not interpreted as fact, but is written as speculation with the best-intended humour applied. This book is not meant to compromise the filmmakers' or artists' vision in any way.

5. And finally – there's no exact science involved. I went to Oxford... well, once, if you count stopping off for petrol at Oxford's Welcome Break Peartree services.

   I'm no scientist, climatologist, astrophysicist, rocket engineer or military expert. The best 'back of a cigarette packet' logic applies throughout this book.

   All scenarios and predictions are however based on sound and logical events, facts, calculations and theories, with references to external sources and articles throughout.

Be more like Janet

So, with all those rules out of the way, it's time to brace for impact and see how we'd truly survive. To quote Morgan Freeman's presidential address in *Deep Impact*: *"So, that's it. Good luck to us all."*

As the sirens wail and the emergency broadcasting system kicks in, all we can do to endure the next series of events is to keep calm, carry on and be more like Janet Elford!

Janet who? You might ask. Janet Elford was made famous overnight in 1996 when she unwittingly appeared on the wind-up TV show *Beadle's About*. Arriving home late one night, she found the authorities on her doorstep and a huge (fibreglass) meteorite in her garden.

Janet famously did the most British thing anyone could do in that situation; she offered an emerging plastic alien a cup of tea! So, throughout the impending doom of the next few chapters, let's all be like Janet, pop that kettle on and keep our upper lips as stiff as we can.

What's the worst that could happen? Well, that would probably all depend on the brand of tea you offered any potential galactic overlord.

Best check the cupboard for *Yorkshire Tea* first or face a horrible, painful death!

TERROR TECHNOLOGY

"In 16 minutes and...oh, 42 seconds the United Kingdom will re-enter the Stone Age" 001

GOLDENEYE

(1995) Dir: Martin Campbell

or almost sixty years, the complex schemes of everyone of James Bond's greatest foes have backfired spectacularly!

From the confines of their hollowed-out volcanic lairs, each villain can intricately plan for almost every inevitability.

But as we well know, it's all completely and utterly pointless. James Bond will always intervene and save the day; it's just what he does!

During the series, the spy extraordinaire has stopped a host of villainous plots ranging from the sublime to the ridiculous.

These include schemes to stir up space race tensions between the USA and USSR in You Only Live Twice (1967), jewel-powered laser satellites in Diamonds Are Forever (1971) and a war between China and the UK to erm... increase TV ratings in Tomorrow Never Dies (1997).

No matter how shaky the plot, 007 has always managed to succeed. But consider this: what would happen if James Bond failed?

With no exploding pens or laser watches to hand, what would the consequences be if the villain triumphed when the end credits rolled?

Bond's seventeenth instalment, *GoldenEye* (1995), stands out as having one of the deadliest of all schemes: the total destruction of London, leaving thousands dead and ramifications for the rest of the UK and the world.

Sounds heavy going, right? Especially for a Bond film. Considering the carnage, when it comes down to it, *GoldenEye* has one of the most understated plot motives, the theft of electronic records from the Bank of England.

Electronic records seem a bit sedate compared to the space race. Still, the planned execution would be anything but, with some downright chilling consequences.

Whilst many threats in the Bond series have remained on the far reaches of fantasy, *GoldenEye* uses a plot device so grounded in reality that it could potentially happen one day. In fact, it's such a threat that I'm reluctant to look it up on Google, as it's considered a highly sensitive subject.

It even made international news in June 2020. A report claimed a special US task force issued an in-depth investigation of China's ability to conduct a "Pearl Harbour style" attack using this technology over US soil. [002]

Campy diamond-powered space lasers, this most certainly isn't! Well, here goes. Wish me luck, and hopefully, I'll see you on the other side, when I get released from prison.

Gulp! Google search: "EMP".

Strike one!

"Now do pay careful attention, 007". EMP, for those who don't know, stands for Electromagnetic Pulse. This short burst of electrical energy wipes out any form of electronic device within a targeted area when released.

First discovered in the 1950s during high altitude nuclear tests, an EMP overloads and destroys any form of electrical-based technology. All devices and mechanisms that use batteries, wires, circuits or microchips are rendered useless.

The strike from an EMP weapon wouldn't directly harm a human per se; however, casualties and death rates would soar from the sheer amount of indirect damage. Anything from pacemakers to nuclear power stations are at risk.

The list is endless and shows our dependency on electronics in this digital age. Dr Pry, an EMP specialist, spoke to *Forbes* magazine in June 2020:

> *"EMPs are one of those things that many people think is fake, or over-blown, or a conspiracy theorist's dream. But they are real. EMPs can be either natural, from things like extreme solar geomagnetic disturbances, or man-made like a large thermonuclear detonation or a cyberattack. If they are coordinated with physical attacks, then things can get real dicey real fast."* [003]

Как активировать Золотой глаз

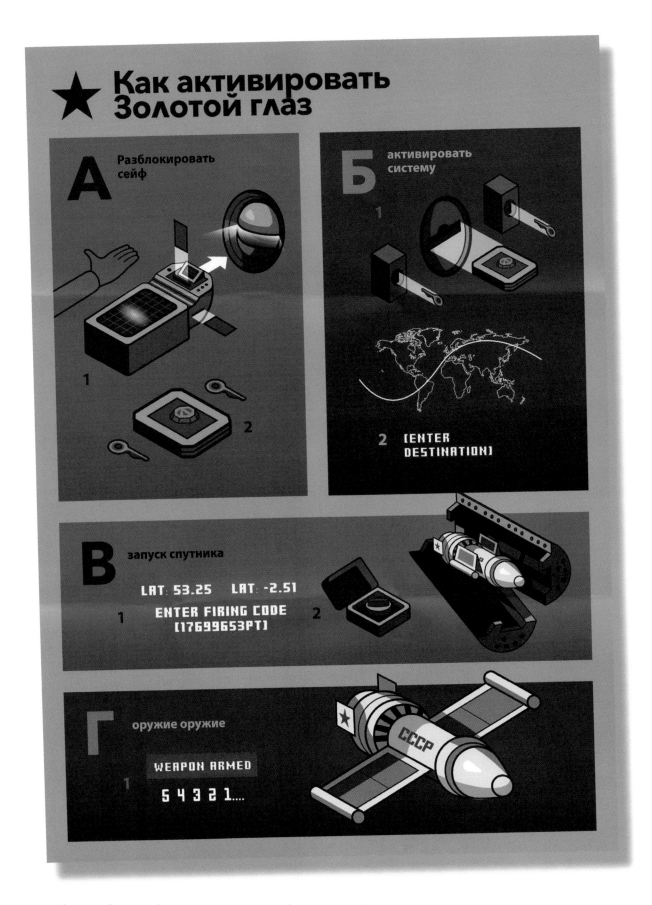

А Разблокировать сейф

1

2

Б активировать систему

1

2 [ENTER DESTINATION]

В запуск спутника

LAT: 53.25   LAT: -2.51

1   ENTER FIRING CODE [17699653PT]   2

Г оружие оружие

WEAPON ARMED

1   5 4 3 2 1....

'Where's the 'any key'? - Instructions on how to start the GoldenEye.

In the film, the EMP device is of course the 'GoldenEye' – a top-secret weapon system made up of two hidden satellites codenamed 'Petya' and 'Mischa'. Developed by the Soviets towards the end of the Cold War, both weapons have been designed to take out an opposing enemy's communications, machinery and weaponry.

The fallout from a 'GoldenEye' attack is only featured on-screen partway through the film, when the 'Petya' satellite strikes Severnaya – a remote Russian space weapons control facility in Siberia.

The strike is revealed to be part of a ruse led by the treacherous General Ourumov (Gottfried John) and his gun-toting leather-clad comrade Xenia Onatopp (Famke Janssen). They aim to steal the controls of the remaining satellite and cover up its theft by destroying the facility in the process. No witness is left alive as all the facility staff are gunned down (00:31:00).

In the turmoil, a distress alarm is activated. Ourumov and Onatopp swiftly make their escape via helicopter as three nearby Russian MIGs are dispatched to investigate.

Unbeknownst to the pair, they have missed one important witness, computer programmer Natalya Simonova (Izabella Scorupco), who emerges out of hiding just as the 'GoldenEye' satellite counts down to target the facility.

At the same time over at MI6 headquarters in London, Bond (Pierce Brosnan), M (Judi Dench) and staff member Tanner (Michael Kitchen) remotely view all the events as they unfold using a live satellite feed.

As the weapon is activated, an electromagnetic pulse blasts outwards for several miles around the facility (00:37:00). Monitors and control panels explode as everywhere goes dark.

The three investigating MIGs suddenly lose power and fall out of the sky; two collide into one another, whilst the third slams directly into the weapons control facility. Miraculously, Simonova manages to break free from the rubble and destruction.

Even the satellite that Bond and the MI6 team are watching the 'live events' on is wiped out by the EMP blast. It's soon revealed that the 'GoldenEye' neutralised all electrical devices within a 30-mile radius of the facility.

The rest of the film follows Bond as he is dispatched by M to find who took the 'GoldenEye' and to stop them. On his globe-trotting mission, he soon uncovers a plot by a former M16 agent, Alec Trevelyan (Sean Bean) to use the remaining 'GoldenEye' satellite to attack London and steal transaction records from the Bank of England.

To quote Trevelyan, his ultimate aim is to *"Have more money than God!"* and *"take the United Kingdom back to the Stone Age"*.

Along the way, Bond partners with Severnaya survivor, Simonova. With the help of an exploding pen and some nifty computer hacking, the remaining 'Mischa GoldenEye' satellite is intercepted and dragged off course, where it breaks up in the atmosphere.

As you'd expect, eventually Trevelyan is killed, Bond gets the girl and London is saved without ever even knowing it was in any danger in the first place.

Cue some dodgy croaky singing by French composer Eric Serra and the credits roll. *"James Bond will return"* is proudly proclaimed at the end. However, consider the consequences if Bond and Simonova had failed on their mission.

Halfway through the film, during the Severnaya EMP attack, Bond states in the MI6 control room, *"No lights. Not one single electric light on in a 30-mile radius."*

In the vast frozen terrains of deepest, darkest Siberia, such an attack probably wouldn't be much of a problem, as your nearest neighbour would probably be 30 miles away or more.

However, compare that to an attack in central London and the effects could be devastating. There would be no end to the carnage and thousands of potential deaths.

So, let's take a look at the possible scale of destruction. I just hope your teeth are in good condition, as let's just say, you might not be using your electric toothbrush for a very long time to come.

From 'The Jetsons' to 'The Flintstones'

The last thing any Brit needs to be mocked for is a lack of dental hygiene; our reputation is bad enough as it is! Pearly whites aside, toothbrushes might be the least of our problems if the 'GoldenEye' were to strike the capital.

As the villainous Alec Trevelyan declares:

> *"It's not just erasing bank records. It's everything on every computer in London. Tax records, the stock market, credit ratings, land registries, criminal records."*

These events were set during the heady pre-broadband and mobile days of 1995, so there would be a total lack of online backups and the cloud facilities that we have today.

The main damage would be far more severe than just missing data. According to the film, the EMP would be around 30 miles in radius, in terms of scale. So if the Bank of England was ground zero, the blast radius would spread out across all of central London and swathes of southeast England, stretching as far as Stevenage in the north, Maidenhead in the east, Crawley in the south and the Essex border in west.

The physical damage on first inspection would be only slight. In the film, there were a few overly exaggerated monitor explosions, but for the most part, it would be a typical power blackout.

However, unlike normal power blackouts, all cars and public transport would cease to work, whilst all portable electrical items would be rendered useless. Probably best to avoid taking the lift and use the stairs instead.

In most standard power blackouts, places like hospitals would have backup generators to restore critical power. However, in an EMP strike, every single electrical item, including the generators, would be taken out.

So 'this is London's problem?' I hear you coldly say

This could mean no life support in any affected hospitals, causing hundreds more deaths. People could also be trapped or locked in structures. Take the London Underground for instance; imagine being stranded in the dark, deep below the surface, trapped in a concrete labyrinth with no lights or means to get out.

However the main danger for anyone caught in the blast zone would come from above. Hundreds of planes would immediately lose power and drop like stones out of the sky.

With five major airports in the London Metropolitan area alone, anyone caught living under the various flight paths around the city is destined to have a very bad day indeed. Thousands more on the ground could die as a result. I would rather take my chances stuck on the underground that day.

The only form of protection to save any electrical goods would be to have kind some of Faraday cage. This would isolate the EMP from damaging any circuitry. Though great in principle, unless you have a Faraday cage the size of a Ford Fiesta, then it's probably not worth the effort.

'So this is London's problem?' I hear you coldly say. However if the 'GoldenEye' were to strike in real life, it would be pretty disastrous for the rest of the UK and the world too.

First of all, the Government would go into meltdown. Power, communications and transport infrastructures would be brought to their knees. Food supply shortages would ricochet across the nation.

The financial and economic impact would be catastrophic; think about how many companies are based in London. Stock markets would crash, and the economic downturn would spread globally, potentially plunging everywhere into a deep global recession.

The only solace to take from *GoldenEye* is that it took place back in a less technology dependant 1995, where the main technological concerns were trying to keep your CD collection scratch-free or avoiding dropping your Game Boy on the kitchen tiles. Back then, there was no Wi-Fi, no smartphones and no ruddy Tik-Tok.

If the strike happened today, it could spark a whole range of modern-day problems ranging from missing Ocado deliveries to failed Uber pickups and mass boredom from social media shutdown.

When Alex Trevelyan said that the UK would re-enter the Stone Age, he meant it. It would be like going from *The Jetsons* to *The Flintstones* in a matter of seconds.

In light of an EMP attack being a real-life threat, it fills you with a sense of dread knowing that James Bond and his world of exploding stationery would not be there to save the day.

I don't know about you, but I'm off to see a man about a Faraday cage.

Scenario

The following worst-case scenario is predicted from events in the film. As only some of the following events were depicted on-screen, logic and rough estimations are applied.

1 The Mischa satellite would strike Central London at around 17:00 on an undetermined date in April 1995. The EMP would spread out across a 30-mile radius, affecting all of central London and swathes of southeast England.

2 Anything electrical would immediately cease to work. There might be minor localised explosions from machinery and electronic goods. All digital records including banking, judicial and financial registries would be wiped out.

3 Cars, trains, buses and all other forms of transport would stop dead. Any planes flying high above the capital would lose power and fall to Earth, exploding on impact. This could kill thousands of passengers on board and people on the ground.

4 Hospitals would no longer have any power. All emergency back-up generators would fail. Hundreds of patients on life- support could potentially die.

5 Government control would crumble. Transport, power and logistic infrastructures around the UK would buckle under the strain, leading to food shortages and unrest across the nation. It could take decades to replace the destroyed technological infrastructure.

6 The surrounding unaffected areas in the South East would become engulfed by people fleeing the capital. This would trigger a mass humanitarian crisis.

7 The financial cost would be devastating for the whole of the UK. This one event would spark a mass global recession, lasting for years in the wake of the events.

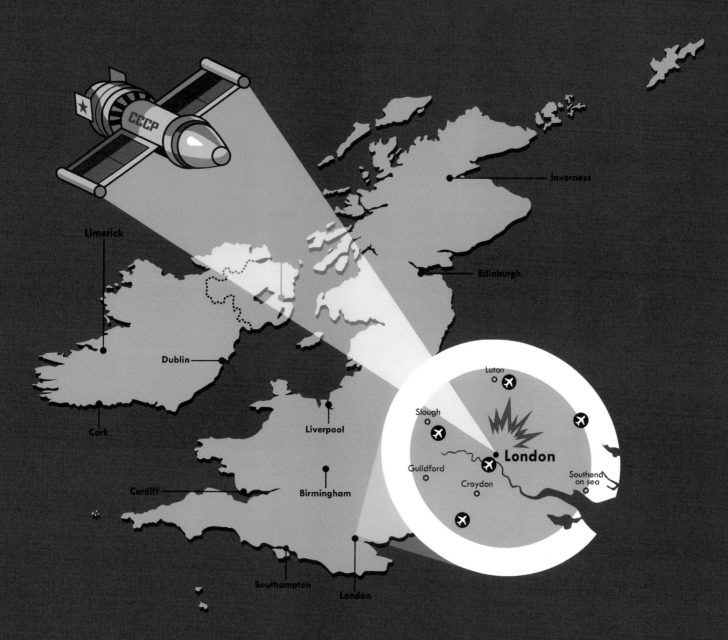

Survival outlook

To be completely honest, it's not looking good for anyone living in London or the South East. The EMP would only last a matter of seconds, but in those few short moments, the devastation would last a lifetime.

The immediate devastation, especially from hundreds of falling planes, would be a total nightmare.

However anyone living beyond the capital would definitely look less smug, as the long-term economic prospects would be disastrous for the entire country. The UK would be decimated and on its knees in a way not seen since the Second World War.

Instead, let's be thankful and raise a Vodka Martini glass to James Bond for always intervening and saving the day. Let's also down those drinks incredibly quickly and pour ourselves another, as we try to put this all too real threat firmly to the back of our minds.

"It started off as rioting. But right from the beginning you knew this was different, because it was happening in small villages, market towns... and then it wasn't on TV anymore. It was on the street outside." 004

28 DAYS LATER

(2002) Dir: Danny Boyle

I t says something about the state of horror movies back in the 1990s, when the only memorable zombie film of the entire decade was *Weekend at Bernie's II* (1993)!

The zombie genre as we knew it was firmly dead and buried in the cynical '90s.

Perhaps *The Macarena*, shell-suits or even the whiff of Lynx Africa were all considered the equivalent of a silver bullet or crucifix to zombies?

One thing's for sure, the zombie genre had long run its course from the vivid crimson gore glory days of the '70s and '80s. Back then, George Romero's classics, *Night of the Living Dead* (1968), *Dawn of the Dead* (1978) and *Day of the Dead* (1985) captured the public's imagination.

Low budget, but nevertheless shocking, these films ruled at the box office. Beneath the surface, they also made profound social commentaries on major issues including the Civil Rights movement, consumerism and the threat of nuclear war.

The 'thick and quick' zombie make-up was re-applied to other films like *Bloodsuckers from Outer Space* (1984), *Return of the Living Dead* (1985), *Dead Heat* (1988) and *I was a Teenage Zombie* (1987), which all copied and cashed in on the craze.

Many of these low-budget horrors however would prove to be hollow experiences, with much of the focus going on the campy schlock aspects, and little or nothing to say about the world around them. These were literal pale imitations in comparison to Romero's films.

By the time the '90s dawned, zombies were no longer seen to be relevant or scary. Their slow-moving dragging feet just couldn't keep up with the fast-changing pace of the modern world around them.

The revival of ironic slasher films like *Scream* (1996) and *I Know What You Did Last Summer* (1997) had taken over the horror mantle. Zombies had silently shuffled their way back into the graveyard and shut the crypt door behind them.

However, as everyone knows, like in all good zombie films, the dead don't stay down for long. As the new millennium dawned, the world had become a more complicated and fearful place. Terrorism, cloning, chemical weapons and a general suspicion of technology had taken hold.

Society had once again become fertile ground for zombies to return and rise up once more. Curiously, it wasn't the Cineplex that first jolted the genre back to life, but the games console. Horror based shoot-em-up games like *Doom* (1993) and *Resident Evil* (1996) were massive hits.

Maverick director of *Trainspotting* (1996), Danny Boyle, and writer of *The Beach* (2000), Alex Garland, took this opportunity for a new take on the zombie film for the 21st century.

Garland, speaking to *FilmMaker* magazine in 2003, commented:

> *"Lots of stuff was happening in this country that felt like the right kind of social subtext or social commentary that you could put in a science fiction film.*
>
> *Danny [Boyle] was particularly interested in issues that had to do with social rage – the increase of rage in our society, road rage and other things. Also, our government's inability to deal with things like BSE (mad cow disease), Foot and Mouth. You always felt that if a virus exploded into our country, our government would be 20 steps behind wherever the virus was."* [005]

28 Days Later (2002) was a low budget, gritty, harrowing and all too real update of the zombie genre. The now iconic scenes of a deserted London remain vividly haunting all these years later. They instantly set a disturbingly desolate and dystopian tone.

The zombies were angrier, more athletic and genuinely more terrifying than their slipper shuffling 80s counterparts

The word zombie isn't mentioned in the film. Instead, they are referred to as 'The Infected'; technically they aren't even dead. Instead, they're victims of a highly contagious genetically modified virus known as 'Rage'.

Here, the zombies were angrier, more athletic and genuinely more terrifying than their slipper-shuffling '80s counterparts. This approach enabled Boyle and Garland to update the genre with no previous expectations and throw the long-established diet of 'zombie brains' out of the window.

For such a small-scale film, *28 Days Later* had a vision on an epic scale. This would become the template for all modern zombie films. Today you can't move for the popularity of zombies, and this is predominantly down to this film.

A sequel followed in 2007 (*28 Weeks Later*), expanding the lore of the film further. It was bigger and more action-packed. However, it lacked some of the vulnerability and fear of the unknown of the original. The *Resident Evil* film franchise also started in 2002, and while not as serious as *28 Days Later*, its popularity led to six sequels, ending in 2016.

Other serious contenders included a remake of *Dawn of the Dead* (2004), updated with new and improved running zombies!

Will Smith's *I Am Legend* (2007) followed a few years later. Whilst it captured some sense of the vulnerability and isolation of *28 Days Later*, the film ruined it all by featuring some truly awful CGI zombies.

More pixelated corpses followed in Brad Pitt's horror actioner *World War Z* (2013). What happened to good old fashioned face paint and fake blood?!

28 Days Later also inspired spin-off genres including the "zom-com" and the "zom-rom-com" with the likes of the now classic *Shaun of the Dead* (2004), *Zombieland* (2009) and *Warm Bodies* (2013).

Other zombie mashups included a Jane Austen adaptation in *Pride and Prejudice and Zombies* (2016), Nazi zombies in *Dead Snow* (2009) and erm… an *EastEnders*-inspired mashup in *Cockneys Versus Zombies* (2012).

The small screen exploded to life too with non-stop zombies, including the seminal series *The Walking Dead* (2010–) and, of course, *Game of Thrones* (2011–2019). For just how long this zombie craze will carry on for is far from well-known.

The legacy of *28 Days Later* will live on, not just as a great horror film but also as a great British film full stop.

After nearly twenty years of going strong, the film only shows some slight signs of decay; it was originally shot using standard definition camcorders, giving it a low-grade quality compared to its ultra-definition contemporaries. Despite this, *28 Days Later* is a zombie film that can still claw, bite and snarl its way to the very top and will always be considered the "patient zero" of modern zombie films.

All the 'Rage'

28 Days Later begins when a group of activists break into a Cambridge animal testing lab and are attacked by a highly infectious caged chimpanzee.

The activists all quickly become infected with the 'Rage virus' and ultimately cause a pandemic to spread like wildfire across the UK.

The film picks up 28 days later and follows Jim (Cillian Murphy), an injured bike courier, who after a road accident awakens from a coma inside a deserted London Hospital (00:08:00).

As he stumbles around a breathtakingly decimated and eerily quiet capital, to Jim's confusion and utter horror, he discovers that he is no longer alone. The city is now teeming with disease-ravaged zombies.

Along the way Jim teams up with a rag-tag group of survivors including Selena (Naomie Harris) and cab driver Frank (Brendan Gleeson) and his daughter Hannah (Megan Burns).

Selena coldly reveals to Jim that whilst he was asleep the entire country succumbed to a deadly and highly infectious pandemic.

Safety first! - protect yourself from being bitten or scratched. Avoid all infected blood and saliva.

She explains:

"It started as rioting. But right from the beginning you knew this was different. Because it was happening in small villages, market towns. And then it wasn't on the TV anymore. It was in the street outside. It was coming in through your windows."

Selena states that all it takes is just one bite, scratch or drop of blood for a person to become struck down by the virus and become one of 'The Infected' (00:18:00).

She also reveals that the entire country has been left in a state of exodus, with the majority of the population fleeing in desperation. There is no government or infrastructure. Any remaining survivors are left to fend for themselves.

With next to no hope of survival in London, the group decides to flee the capital when they hear a radio broadcast from a group of soldiers on the outskirts of Manchester. It beckons any survivors to come to their outpost, where they will be protected and cared for (00:40:00). The group soon pack up some supplies and travel up north in Frank's black cab.

On eventual arrival to the outskirts of Manchester (now in flames), the survivors stumble upon a deserted military outpost (00:59:00).

As they explore the area, disaster strikes when Frank becomes infected from a single drop of blood to his eye (01:03:00). Just as Frank begins to turn he is shot and killed by a group of emerging camouflaged soldiers.

Under escort, Jim, Selena and Hannah are quickly taken to a commandeered manor house where they are introduced to squad leader Major Henry West (Christopher Eccleston).

As the three survivors soon discover, all is not as it seems. To their horror it's revealed that the radio broadcast was all part of a ploy to lure survivors and begin a twisted re-population program.

As Selena and Hannah are held captive, Jim is taken out in the woods to be executed. He however soon outwits the soldiers and quickly returns back to the manor house in a bid to rescue the girls.

Jim takes bloody revenge on the soldiers (01:30:00) when he releases a chained infected soldier known as "Private Mailer", who has been kept for observation, into the mansion.

Chaos and screams echo throughout the hallways as the soldiers one by one quickly fall victim to "Private Mailer". A heavily injured Jim manages to rescue Selena and Hannah and they all flee the manor house in their taxi. Jim however soon falls unconscious in the back seat and the screen turns to black.

Another 28 days pass, where it's revealed the three survivors have been living in a remote cottage in the Lake District (01:41:00).

The film ends as they run outside and piece together a giant "SOS banner" out on lawn. This captures the attention of a low-flying Finnish air force jet that soars overhead.

Ready-made zombie!

The events of *28 Days Later* would be absolutely cataclysmic in the UK. Recently the film has taken on a whole new meaning, as it's been somewhat a dark mirror to the global events of the 2020 pandemic.

28 Days Later is probably the one film in this entire book where the events are all too relatable. Reviewed in context, some of the events from the film are now downright chilling.

If this were to happen in reality, the sense of dread, panic and confusion would be all too familiar. Although, I'm not so sure toilet rolls would become such an essential item in Danny Boyle's universe.

Worryingly, as the title suggests, it takes just 28 days after the first Cambridge lab incident for the entire UK mainland to become consumed by the 'Rage virus'. The virus is so rapid that it takes approximately 10–30 seconds for a healthy person to become infected and transform into a zombie.

All it takes is one bite, scratch or transmission of blood or saliva, as the character Frank discovers to his fate (01:03:00).

This rapid rate of infection does have a positive side though. Of course, it's bad news if you've been bitten, but, the quick zombie transformation time (one minute or less) would make it easy to distinguish between the infected and other healthy humans.

In most zombie films (pre-2002), the victim to zombie transition time was much slower. An average zombie transformation could take anywhere from one hour to half a day. A victim would appear to be normal, if only getting clammy and eventually turning grey. None the less they would easily be able to blend in with society.

The *28 Days Later* infection changes this trope. One minute or less and ping: you're a full-on ready-made zombie! This would make it easier to separate the infected and make it much more difficult for the infection to spread across the country.

For example, imagine you're in a traditional zombie film and bitten outside Manchester Piccadilly station. You then board the five-hour

And stay out! - How the French border could possibly look. "Zone de quarantaine stricte. Tireurs D'Élite" ("Strict quarantine area. Snipers").

train to Bournemouth. Then during that time you could likely travel across much of the country without ever fully transforming into a zombie.

You would probably start to feel clammy as you read your *Take a Break* magazine and had your tea and shortbread from the trolley. Then only as you'd pull into Bournemouth station would you start to be craving human brains for dinner.

However, in *28 Days Later*, there's no chance that such a train would even leave the station, or if it did there would be a high likelihood of an emergency cord being pulled.

The only way for the infection to spread would be if the train was a super-fast direct service to London (like in the 2016 Korean film *Train to Busan*). Though how far the train would make it down the tracks, I'm not sure.

If basic humans have enough trouble using the door buttons on the *Star Trek*-style toilets onboard Pendolino trains, I'm not sure they would prevent highly energetic zombies from sneaking down the line undetected.

Another difference between *28 Days Later* and older zombie films is here the zombies can run, and boy are they fast! Compared to previous incarnations, the zombies are quicker, more accurate and much more deadly. They can even climb stairs and overcome basic obstacles (00:32:00).

Like in all good zombie films, 'The Infected' share some generic traits and weaknesses with their zombie predecessors. They don't possess high levels of intelligence or direction and are completely aimless.

One kiss, touch or even sneeze could be all it takes

The only way to draw their attention is with light, noise, or movement. In *28 Days Later*, 'The Infected' are considered to be hypersensitive. For example, in one scene, when Jim looks through some old family photos in his kitchen, he holds candlelight around the room.

This one dim light is enough to draw the attention of two 'Infected', as they crash through the kitchen conservatory with all the vigour of an SAS squadron (00:26:00).

If introduced to highly populated areas, 'The Infected' could easily overcome town and city centres within hours. In inter-connected metropolitan areas like the West Midlands, containing cities like Coventry, Birmingham and Wolverhampton, the virus could spread within days, as 'The Infected' could easily roam through the urban corridor from one area to another.

Areas with rural boundaries separating towns and cities stand a better chance of protection. 'The Infected' wouldn't as easily venture into quieter areas. There would be fewer distractions, harsher landscapes and smaller, more widespread populations to get their teeth around.

That said, I'd hold off any plans to attend outdoor concerts or firework displays for the time being. Glastonbury would definitely be off that year.

The movement of 'The Infected' would be the equivalent of setting fire to doused petrol on a street. This would burn instantly and ferociously in the spilt areas, but not spread as easily to the drier parts.

Remote cities like Exeter, Plymouth, Inverness and Norwich would all stand a better chance of being infection free, but this certainly would not be guaranteed.

The safest places in the British Isles by far would be any areas separated by water. The Irish mainland, the Isle of Man, Isle of Wight, the Channel Islands, the Shetlands and parts of the Scottish Hebrides would all stand a better chance of holding back the infection.

France and Holland too would be considered safe zones, with the virus not escaping from the UK. This is confirmed in the 2007 sequel *28 Weeks Later*. Still, all these areas would forever be on a daily knife-edge; if just one of 'The Infected' were to break through quarantine, it would mean certain doom for that area.

After the mass exodus mentioned in the film (00:18:00), strict controlled quarantine borders would probably be set-up across the Irish Sea, North Sea and English Channel, with each nation's respective armed forces holding back any unauthorised boats and aircraft.

The subject of astigmatic infections is brought up in the sequel *28 Weeks Later*, and though not featured in this film, it could act as ultimate 'trojan horse' to take down safe zones.

Considered rare, asymptomatic patients could carry the virus unwittingly across quarantined borders.

One kiss, touch or even sneeze could be all it takes to flare up the virus and re-infect the population. As a result, safe or infection-free zones would be on a constant state of alert.

If you were unfortunate enough to miss the exodus from the mainland, there is still hope. But you'd need to be well prepared and be in it for the long haul. If you made it to the countryside with lots of supplies, stayed low and kept all noise, movement and light to a minimum, you could probably protect yourself and outlive 'The Infected'.

That's probably easier said than done though. If I were in that situation, I would have drained all my supplies within the first week and ventured outside to desperately search for KitKat Chunkys, cider or Wotsits. Bear Grylls, I am sadly not.

Towards the end of the film, another 28 days pass. On-screen, we see an emaciated zombie in the Lake District, slumped on the floor and gawping up as a military jet passes above.

This shows that in the near 60 days since the outbreak began, 'The Infected' would be starting to die off. However, it would be a safe bet to hold back from hosting any impromptu candle-lit suppers by your front window for the time being.

If you can make it an additional 168 days, by which time the sequel begins, you'll be considered very lucky indeed.

However that too will probably end up in 'asymptomatic infectious tears', as by the time the sequel concludes, SPOILER ALERT, let's just say it doesn't end well for anyone!

Scenario

The following worst-case scenario is predicted from events in the film. As only some of the following events were depicted on-screen, logic and rough estimations are applied.

1 The Rage virus would break out of a Cambridge Lab after an infected chimpanzee is released by a group of animal rights activists. The animal attacks the activists and infects them with the Rage virus.

2 Without any warning, 'The Infected' would engulf the surrounding area and attack swathes of the local population. The virus would spread rapidly as victims "Run, attack, infect and repeat".

3 Confusion, fear, and panic would take hold as the virus expands across the country. Once reaching highly populated areas, it would spread like wildfire.

4 It would overwhelm emergency services and local government agencies.

5 The UK Armed Forces would try to strike back, but would be powerless to stop the spread.

6 The Government and society would eventually collapse as more people become infected.

7 Strict quarantine controls would come into place as evacuees try to get off shore to the following areas: the Irish mainland, the Shetlands, the Hebrides, the Channel Islands, the Isle of Man, the Isle of Wight, France or the Netherlands and beyond.

8 All land, sea and air borders would close as the mainland UK eventually becomes quarantined. No-go zones would be controlled by foreign armed forces.

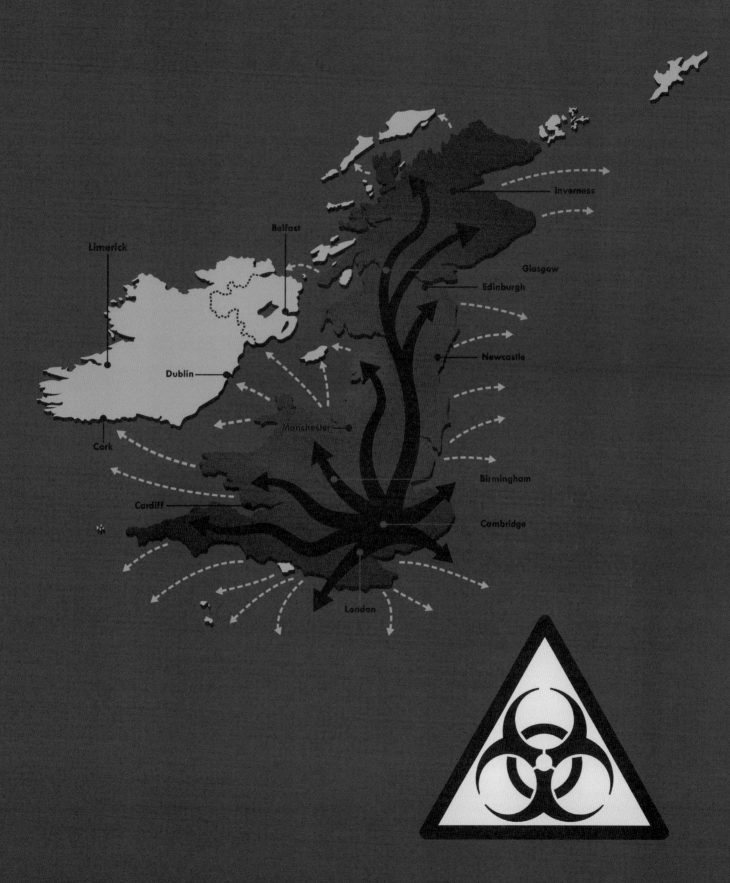

Survival outlook

Anyone living on the Irish mainland or islands off the UK will be breathing a heavy sigh of relief. There would be a high possibility of remaining infection-free in these areas; however, it would be a long, precarious wait. Society would crumble if just one of 'The Infected' were to sneak through a barricade or become shipwrecked on a beach.

Anyone left on the UK mainland is probably going to have to endure a few miserable difficult months. Parts of the countryside and remote towns and cities might fare better, but again this is no guarantee of staying infection-free.

My best advice is to relocate to the countryside and wait for the remaining 'Infected' to die off. It might take a while, so make sure you have some good books and board games to hand. Stay low, stay silent, and I'd strongly recommend that you keep your running shoes handy by the front door.

"Mankind is the virus, and I am the cure". ₀₀₆

KINGSMAN: THE SECRET SERVICE

(2015) Dir: Matthew Vaughn

Tnight it's the night of the big regional premiere of *Quantum of Solace* in Chester, England. The atmosphere is positively electric. However, beyond the red carpet glitz and glamour, not everyone is revelling with the same degree of enthusiasm.

"Ejector seats! Not heated seats!"
"Sidewinders! Not Satnavs!"

These were just some of the placards that greeted the glamorous guests (including Daniel Craig's Dad) outside the Cineworld multiplex.

As reported by *Cheshire-live.co.uk*, [007] this protest, led by some highly passionate James Bond fans, raised concerns about how the

"Ejector seats! Not heated seats!"

"Sidewinders! Not Satnavs!"

series had started to become overtly corporate and take itself way too seriously. Spokesman Vernon Kerswell stated:

"We're not anti-Bond, in fact, we're massive Bond fans – but we don't like the new serious Bond and want to see him lighten up".

The group of light-hearted protestors may have been small in size, but they definitely had a valid point. To coin a phrase from *Austin Powers*, the Daniel Craig era of Bond films were at risk of losing some of their 'mojo'.

Re-launched two years previously with the global box office smash, *Casino Royale* (2006), the Daniel Craig era brutally wiped the slate clean of the previous 'final fantasy' mess-up that was *Die Another Day* (2002).

Gone were the ice palaces, invisible cars and notorious CGI surfing that had pushed the series to a state of near self-parody. Even Bond legend Sir Roger Moore said in an interview with *Entertainment Weekly* [008] in 2008:

"I thought that [Die Another Day] was a bit phantasmagoric – invisible cars! They went too far."

For this statement to come from the only Bond to go up into outer space really says something.

The Bond series' reinvention took inspiration from a new era of much tougher and realistic spy films, mainly Matt Damon's kinetic and fast-paced *Bourne Identity* (2002) and *Bourne Supremacy* (2004).

The Bond franchise as a result was rejuvenated with a more relatable and modern action hero. Craig's Bond was far more emotional and human. The action scenes too, were grounded in reality, but still remained spectacular and bruise-inducing.

Casino Royale was by far one of the most serious adaptations of Ian Fleming's super spy. This new dramatic edge to the Bond series also took it a step away from some of the series' previous more outlandish elements.

Out went the gadgets and gone were the majority of puns; there was no danger of an invisible car reappearing in this world! Craig would follow-up as Bond in the aforementioned *Quantum of Solace* (2008).

Despite the success, at this point in the series there was a distinct feeling that the sense of fun and many classic Bond elements were unnecessarily being thrown out with the bath water. There was no time for gags or faffing around with Vodka Martinis in this new era.

One person who could probably sympathise with the Chester protesters was visionary director of *Stardust* (2007), *Kick Ass* (2010) and *X-Men: First Class* (2011), Matthew Vaughn. He, too, thought that spy films were getting slightly more serious.

One drunken conversation in a pub would lead to the birth of a whole new spy franchise. Speaking to *Gizmodo.com* [009] in 2015, Vaughn remarked:

> "It started in a pub with Mark [Millar, author of comic Kick-Ass] and we were drunk. And we sort of were complaining about how spy movies had become really quite serious. We said, 'Let's do a fun one.' We were really drunk. 'God, we did this, we did that,' and then Mark went off and wrote a version [of Kingsman], and I read it. I was like, 'Fuck, maybe we should do this for real.'

The Kingsman: The Secret Service (2015) was a new unapologetically British take on the spy genre. It was a unique blend of ultra-violent cinema and all the cheekiness that the Roger Moore-era Bond films had proudly worn on their safari suit jacket sleeves. The film stuck two fingers up at the grittiness of the *Jason Bourne* films.

Produced in the mould of camp '60s spy shows like *The Man from U.N.C.L.E* and *The Avengers*, *The Kingsman* introduced a highly secret organisation, led behind the scenes from an exclusive tailor's in Savile Row, London.

The film was a wild ride with exhilarating action sequences that ditched a lot of the Craig era films' seriousness. The pretentiousness was gone, but back were all gadgets and cheeky fun that the Bond films once held dear.

The Kingsman had emotion and heart and covered many deep topics including privilege and fatherhood. But it still had time to make you laugh and shock you too, such as the now infamous anal sex scene (01:59:00).

You could hardly imagine the classic *Moonraker* line, *"I think he's attempting re-entry, Sir"* being said in one of Daniel Craig's Bond films. Yet this line could easily sit snugly within *The Kingsman* series.

The film also modernises the 'Global domination' plot that became the figure of fun in the *Austin Powers* films. *The Kingsman* cleverly uses our weakness for heavily discounted phone bills against us in a plan involving free sim cards and mind control. Sounds totally over the top. Right?

However, when you compare this to the plot of *Quantum of Solace*, involving the ransom of Bolivia's water supply (seriously, that was the plot!), I know which one I'd rather watch! No wonder people were protesting outside the cinema at the time.

The Kingsman was a massive global success, raking in $414m globally and lead to sequels *Kingsman: The Golden Circle (2017)* and *The King's Man* (2021). The film breathed new life into the spy genre and even gave old 007 a run for his money. Not bad at all for a movie written after a few pints down at the pub.

'Valentine's' Day

The storyline follows troubled South London teen Gary "Eggsy" Unwin (Taron Egerton). He is taken under the wing of gentleman super-spy Harry Hart (Colin Firth), a member of the top-secret organisation, The Kingsman. Seeing potential in Eggsy, Harry puts him through months of gruelling training for a position within the organisation.

Deadly data bundle - A mock-up of one Valentine's marketing campaigns. Subject to a lifetime contract guarantee.

Harry meanwhile follows clues left after the mysterious disappearance of a scientist and death of a fellow Kingsman agent.

Harry is eventually led to the door of illustrious tech billionaire, Richmond Valentine, played with great relish by the brilliant Samuel L. Jackson.

Alongside his deadly assistant, an assassin with bladed prosthetic legs know as Gazelle (Sofia Boutella), Valentine's plan is soon revealed. He plots to cull the global population in a bid to stop mankind's wanton destruction of the environment (01:28:00). He reveals:

"When you get a virus, you get a fever. That's the human body raising its core temperature to kill the virus. Planet Earth works the same way: Global warming is the fever; mankind is the virus.

We're making our planet sick. A cull is our only hope. If we don't reduce our population ourselves, there's only one of two ways this can go: The host kills the virus, or the virus kills the host. Either way..."

His grand scheme is to give away millions of his new phone SIM cards, with the promise of free calls and free internet for everyone in the world forever.

The Kingsmen soon uncover that the SIM cards conceal a deadly secret; they carry a hidden signal that, once activated, turns anyone nearby into a mindless homicidal maniac. Valentine meets with the world's wealthy and powerful and offers them an ultimatum.

In return for their cooperation, Valentine gives them a surgical procedure to the back of the neck, where a tiny immunity implant is inserted. This device counteracts the effects of the signal, making the elite immune to the upcoming cull. Anyone unwilling to cooperate is imprisoned in the confines of Valentine's secret mountainous base.

As Harry digs deeper, he falls into a trap at an infamous hate preaching church in Kentucky where he is unknowingly exposed to a short-range test of Valentine's cull signal. A brutal massacre soon ensues. When Harry eventually comes to his senses, he is ambushed outside the church and shot in the head by Valentine (01:23:00).

Eggsy, fellow Kingsman recruit Roxy (Sophie Cookson), and Technical Operative Merlin (Mark Strong), hatch a plan to find Valentine and stop him before it's all too late.

In a bid to delay the cull, Roxy is assigned to destroy one of Valentine's satellites. She takes a special high altitude balloon into the stratosphere, where she dutifully fires a rocket (01:43:00). Eggsy and Merlin infiltrate Valentine's "End of the World" party, held at his secret mountainous hideout, attended by dignitaries and the elite.

Eggsy's cover is blown, and he ends up fighting hordes of heavily armed guards. Cornered and outnumbered, he gets the idea to reverse the frequency of the implants. Merlin activates the signal to its maximum strength. Without warning, all of the guards' heads blow up. Leaders and dignitaries across the world get their just desserts, as their heads also gleefully explode on-screen to the tune of 'Land of Hope and Glory' (01:48:00).

The inhabitants of every country around world would be at each other's throats

An angry Valentine soon restores his satellite signal and proceeds with his plan. Through biometric security settings, he places his hand on a control pad and activates the worldwide cull.

Within seconds phones across the world are activated with the deadly signal. As gruesomely displayed earlier, anyone close to a handset becomes an out of control homicidal manic. People across the globe violently attack one another.

After 1 minute 25 seconds of global chaos, the cull is temporarily halted when Eggsy storms in to the control room with a machine gun. Gazelle fights back, allowing Valentine to restart the cull by placing his hand back on the controls.

Millions are injured or killed as the chaos restarts and intensifies (01:53:00). Finally, Eggsy defeats Gazelle and impales Valentine with one of her prosthetic legs. As the cull ceases, people worldwide are left battered and bewildered (01:56:00).

Eggsy rescues a captured Swedish princess (Hanna Alström) in a 'cheeky' nod to the Roger Moore Bond humour of years ago in one of the final scenes.

'I Predict a Riot'

Cheeky bum sex aside, the consequences of Valentine's plan of a global mass homicide would be catastrophic.

On-screen, in the combined time of nearly 4 ½ minutes, the inhabitants of every country around world would be at each other's throats. It's not really possible to know the full extent of casualties and deaths involved, but it could easily be in the hundreds of thousands, if not millions.

This figure would unquestionably be higher if the Kingsman had failed to stop Valentine. It's particularly chilling in one scene involving Eggsy's mother, Michelle (Samantha Womack). Wielding a knife, she tries to break down a locked bathroom door to kill her own baby on the other side (00:53:00).

Luckily, the signal stops before she bursts into the bathroom in full-on 'Shining mode'. If this same situation were played out elsewhere, it could have far deadlier ramifications. Vulnerable people, including children and the elderly, might not be so lucky.

The fact is, the signal could take over the mind of anyone. You don't even have to have a Valentine SIM card, or own a phone, as others nearby could act as signal beacons. However there are several flaws to Valentine's plan that need addressing. The first being, Valentine uses a ring of satellites to transmit his signal across the globe.

If these were purpose-built satellite phones, the signal would be picked up directly from the satellites. In the film, however, all the devices appear to be bog-standard network phones, with only Valentine's new SIM card inserted as a replacement (00:46:00).

This means all the phones would rely on existing mobile phone network infrastructures, such as signal towers and cables. [010]

The only way to successfully broadcast Valentine's 'cull signal' would be to relay it from the satellites via the existing phone network. Knowing the state of the UK's phone network coverage, you're definitely going to have some gaps in transmission or weak signal coverage in certain areas.

It's a good job Valentine's plans didn't cover Wi-Fi. If this were the case, the death rates would be astronomical.

Poor network areas would be relatively unaffected by the 'cull signal', and those in certain city office blocks might not receive or take calls due to the 'Faraday cage' effect.

Places like the London Underground too, could prove to be a signal-free zone and just well save your life.

To estimate the network coverage and determine what areas would escape the 'cull signal', we need to look at the phone signal area maps from 2015, when the film was released. [011]

As there is no "Valentine network" in reality, the data here is roughly worked out by layering 2015 phone coverage maps (Vodafone, EE, O2 & Three) on top of one another and working out the gaps in between.

As expected, large parts of southwest England, rural Wales, the Pennines, the Irish countryside and the Scottish Highlands would remain largely unscathed.

If you managed to get into a fight down the pub in any of these areas, then it's probably not due to any 'signal'; you've probably sat in the wrong chair or something.

Scenario

The following worst-case scenario is predicted from events in the film. As none of the following events were depicted on-screen, logic and rough estimations are applied throughout.

1 Without warning, Valentine would initiate his global cull. Using satellites and existing phone networks, anyone in possession of a Valentine SIM powered mobile phone would act as a transmitter of the deadly cull signal.

2 Once exposed, anyone nearby would become a homicidal maniac. People would start fighting, attacking or killing for a total of 4 ½ minutes.

3 Anyone in poor signal zones would remain largely unaffected. Areas include: southwest England, rural Wales, the Pennines, the Irish countryside and the Scottish Highlands. Attacks here would be patchy at best.

4 People in large cities with usually great phone network coverage would be the worst affected. Affected areas would include: London, Birmingham, Manchester and Glasgow.

5 People in large office buildings, complexes and underground transport systems would have less exposure to the signal. This would all depend on their location.

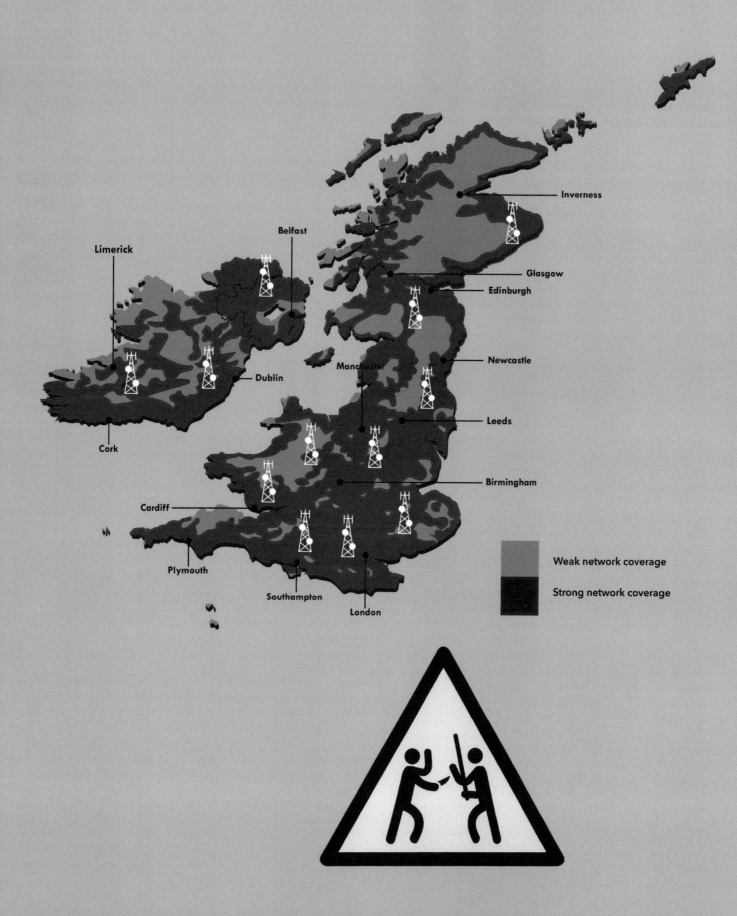

Limerick

Belfast

Inverness

Glasgow

Edinburgh

Cork

Dublin

Newcastle

Manchester

Leeds

Cardiff

Birmingham

Plymouth

Southampton

London

Weak network coverage

Strong network coverage

Survival outlook

It goes against the grain to not want any phone reception. Anyone in the big cities or areas with a great network would pay a heavy price during the global cull. Those in signal blackout areas would be largely unscathed. But, coverage from Valentine's signal might leak through to those areas.

Perhaps a weaker signal could turn you into a lesser sort of maniac: '2G' could lead to heavy tussling? 'E' might be apply to bitchslaps only? Who knows? Either way, the less said about what '5G' can do to you, the better!

ALIEN INVASION

"Now that's what I call a close encounter!" [012]

INDEPENDENCE DAY

(1996) Dir: Roland Emmerich

The Superbowl, to most non-Americans, is a perplexing spectacle.

The big game itself feels like a poor second cousin when up against all the glitz and pageantry of its half-time show and multi-million dollar commercials. You couldn't imagine the latest Vauxhall Zafira advert hogging all the limelight during the FA Cup or Wimbledon.

The events of the 1996 Superbowl proved no different, as the event was overshadowed by something different altogether.

Cut to commercial break: on-screen, a menacing giant spaceship looms over the White House. The landmark is suddenly blown to pieces in a giant fireball. *"Enjoy the Superbowl. It may be your last!"* is slammed on the screen.

No-one in their right mind would be talking about 'football' now surely?

No one in their right mind would be talking about 'football' after seeing this, surely? This 30-second TV spot for a previously unheard-of film caught the attention and imagination of the world. *Independence Day* had been well and truly declared!

Sure, the desecration of national monuments had long been featured on-screen. Look at the shock reveal of the Statue of Liberty in The *Planet of the Apes* (1968), General Zod's White House attack in *Superman 2* (1980) or dare I mention the straightening of the Leaning Tower of Pisa in *Superman 3* (1983). In all these instances, the landmarks had been lovingly played with, yet carefully respected in return.

Independence Day (1996) totally ripped up this rule. To quote *The Simpsons*, [013] when Homer is looking for the largest, most destructive illegal fireworks in a convenience store, the clerk hands him a rocket and remarks:

"Celebrate the independence of your nation by blowing up a small part of it".

This attitude and spirit are perfectly summed up by this film. When the White House is attacked, it's completely obliterated with no hope in hell of getting the decorators back in. The new notion of nothing sacred was refreshing to audiences at the time and had never been seen before.

Alien invasion films up until now had been low-key 'smash and grab' affairs. They mostly involved the abduction of Midwest townsfolk or remained small-scale schemes of global domination.

Films like *The Day the Earth Stood Still* (1951) are iconic, but lacked a great deal of action, while in George Pal's classic *War of the Worlds* (1953), the aliens had no clear plan of invasion, instead choosing to aimlessly hover and zap their way around Southern California.

Director and producer duo, Roland Emmerich and Dean Devlin, modernised this concept by making aliens a genuine global threat. Here, the aliens had a clear battle plan and made an un-nerving grandiose entrance to all of mankind; hovering leviathan spaceships over the Earth's major cities.

To quote the poster, *"The question of whether or not we are alone in the universe has been answered"*, and boy was it answered.

Independence Day was a heady concoction of the adventure of *Star Wars* combined with the jeopardy of 1970s disaster films. Also added to the mix were the shadowy undertones of government conspiracies set by *The X-Files* (1993-2018), topped off with the gloopy sauce of American patriotism.

In the hands of any American director, the levels of patriotism might have been too gung-ho and off-putting, however, German-born Emmerich ladled this mixture lightly, allowing the film not to take itself too seriously.

This winning combination, along with some amazing special effects and the breakout performance of a certain *Fresh Prince*, led *Independence Day* to become a global box office phenomenon.

The film would also go on to briefly inspire the revitalisation of the 'Hollywood Disaster epic' in films such as *Armageddon* (1998), *Deep Impact* (1998) **(pages 95-102)** and *The Core* (2003). This era would however be soon short-lived after the sobering real-life events of 9/11 shocked the world.

Director Roland Emmerich would however plough on with his one-man tirade of destruction. In 2004 he toppled more landmarks in *The Day after Tomorrow* **(pages 103-112)**.

He even took another pop at the White House with a tsunami and an aircraft carrier in the apocalyptic *2012* (2009).

Like its imposing spaceships on-screen, the success of *Independence Day* would influence Hollywood for many years to come. The film has long been imitated but never surpassed.

I struggle at the best of times to get my Bluetooth speakers and iPhone to work together, yet getting a 1996 Apple Mac to speak with an alien spaceship seems strangely possible.

The less said about its 2016 sequel, *Independence Day: Resurgence* **(pages 81–90)** though, the better! It goes to show that, like its namesake, *Independence Day* needs to be declared once and once only!

They're here!

The world takes a collective gasp as several 15-mile-wide spaceships descend through the atmosphere and unnervingly hover above some of the world's largest cities. On-screen, these giant spaceships nestle above landmarks of New York, Washington D.C. and Los Angeles (00:21:09).

As communication attempts with the new arrivals all but fail, TV satellite engineer David Levinson (Jeff Goldblum) discovers a

hidden clue within our satellite system. The aliens are silently counting down towards an attack. Along with his father (Judd Hirsch), Levinson rushes to Washington D.C. to warn his estranged wife Constance (Margaret Colin) of the impending danger. Super conveniently, she also works as the Communications Director for the White House.

She informs President Whitmore (Bill Pullman), who orders the mass evacuation of every major US city. The President, his staff, and Levinson and his father, swiftly escape on board Air Force One (00:50:37). Unfortunately, it's too late for thousands of people left behind as the aliens begin their global attack.

Landmarks are destroyed as an explosive wall of fire ravages across New York, LA and Washington D.C. (00:48:50). After the destruction, the City Destroyers (as the ships become known) move to their next target. At this point, the US Air Force begins their counterattack, with ace fighter pilot Captain Steven Hiller (Will Smith) taking to the skies.

As the military retaliates, they realise that the alien technology is far superior to our feeble weaponry, with each ship having impenetrable shields (00:58:04). It's like they've never seen a science fiction film before!

The City Destroyers unleash thousands of small fighter craft, which massacre the military and wipe out key strategic government and military bases (01:01:18).

Hiller flees, but not without taking down one of the alien fighters, smoking a cigar and making many a wisecrack along on the way. It was the '90s, after all (01:02:30).

All the central characters rally around at a newly declassified Area 51 in the Arizona Desert, where it's revealed that the Government has secretly been storing an old alien fighter, leftover from the infamous 1940s Roswell UFO crash (01:11:30).

Levinson finds a way to beat the aliens by hacking the alien fighter's technology and uploading a Trojan virus into the orbiting mothership to tamper with their defences.

This plot hole has gone down in legend over the years. I struggle at the best of times to get my Bluetooth speakers and iPhone to work together, yet getting a 1996 Apple Mac to speak with an alien spaceship seems strangely possible?

Levinson and Hiller hatch a plan to pilot the captive alien fighter to space, sneak on-board the Mothership and upload the virus (01:41:00).

As the virus is uploaded, groups of fighter pilots across the world strike back at the now vulnerable City Destroyers. One by one, they are all destroyed and blown out of the sky (02:10:00).

Meanwhile, on-board the alien mothership, Levinson and Hiller fire a timed nuclear missile into the vessel. As our heroes make their escape, the clock ticks to zero as a shocked alien looks down at the timer. It explodes, destroying all of the aliens on board (02:15:00).

Humanity is saved, and before you can yankee-doodle dandy, it's the end of the film. Everyone on the ground is smoking cigars, having barbecues and celebrating their victory.

I'm not sure if Norwich would be high on the aliens' hit list. Delia Smith can rest easy.

They look up and rejoice as small fragments of the mothership burn up in the atmosphere (02:18:30).

Despite being portrayed as a global alien invasion, the events of *Independence Day* are purely an American affair, taken from a US perspective only. To be honest, you wouldn't expect it any other way, given the title. However, a couple of scenes towards the end of the film open up a sneak peek at the fate of the rest of the world. These are what I call the "Dancing Ewok" scenes, based on a scene originally featured at the end of *Return of Jedi* (1983).

This showed a montage of rejoicing Ewoks and other characters across the galaxy in joint celebration over the fall of the evil galactic empire. During *Independence Day's* "Dancing Ewok" scenes, we see a collection of downed City Destroyers against the backdrops of the African savannah, Cairo, and Sydney. All scenes featured celebrating locals doing their best green screen rejoicing (02:15:45).

Unfortunately, the UK remains absent from this list, which raises the ultimate question of how we would handle ourselves in such an invasion. Most importantly, would we survive and be celebrating too?

'We come in peace' - A handy do's and don'ts guide to communicating with our alien visitors.

The British Invasion

From the events of *Independence Day*, we know that one of the City Destroyers appears over central London. A news broadcast plays in the background of David's New York satellite TV company's offices. The footage shows a Sky News report (00:26:23) with a City Destroyer hovering above Big Ben.

From the news reports, we can also verify that in addition to London, there are five ships across Europe, hovering over Paris, Berlin, Moscow and Rome (00:27:09).

Based on what happens in the film, we can roughly work out the aliens' plan of attack, but as this isn't featured on-screen the following is made up of theories, predictions and logic.

Like the US cities featured, London would be totally destroyed in a giant fireball. Anyone using the Underground might stand a better chance of survival. This would all depend on how deep you were within the tunnel networks.

Once central London had been wiped out, the aliens would probably next take out the highly populated satellite towns, urban areas and suburbs within the M25 area.

To work out the alien's next probable move, we should look at the population data. Their aim would be to wipe out as many people as possible, quickly and efficiently.

The predicted plan would involve travelling to the highest populated cities [014] in the UK and Ireland, in an order based on their geographical position away from London and their close proximity to one another. Building on this theory, the plan of attack for the first 25 cities would probably be in the following order:

London, Reading, Oxford, Birmingham, Wolverhampton, Derby, Nottingham, Sheffield, Manchester, Liverpool, Dublin, Belfast, Glasgow, Edinburgh, Newcastle, Middlesbrough, Leeds, Leicester, Coventry, Worcester, Gloucester, Bath, Bristol, Cardiff and Swansea.

The route would be the equivalent of a greatest hits tour of the UK and Ireland. Major cities on the far corners of the British Isles like Aberdeen, Plymouth or Cork would probably be least of the aliens' problems.

The invasion plans would however have two major flaws. The first being, after their initial attack on London, the cat would be firmly out of the bag! The first surprise attack that caught out thousands in the capital would not be repeated.

People in all cities and towns would evacuate to the countryside, mountains or coast. The City Destroyers would continue on their path of destruction, but only managing to damage infrastructure and property.

The second flaw is there is only one City Destroyer for the whole of the British Isles, so it would take a while for it to travel on its grand tour. As Robert Loggia's character General Grey declares:

> *"We're looking at the major destruction of every major world city in the next 36 hours"* (01:21:24).

I'm not sure if Norwich would be high on the aliens' hit list. Delia Smith can rest easy. That said, the fate for everyone else is indicated towards the end of the film.

When Hiller and Levinson infiltrate the mothership, on-screen they fly past millions of alien troops lined up in preparation to invade (02:00:30). It's most likely that after the initial City Destroyer attacks cease, the aliens would launch ground troops to round up any survivors.

If the predicted events mirror the film, then the UK Armed Forces would no doubt strike back after London is destroyed. Sadly, they would suffer a similar fate to the US Air Force. Key military bases, government facilities and even royal palaces would be destroyed.

So how does the invasion end? To work this out we need to look twenty years into the future. Despite flopping on its release in 2016, the much-panned sequel, *Independence Day: Resurgence*, played an essential part in filling in the gaps left by the original.

This doesn't occur in the film itself, but rather in its marketing. *Warof1996.com* was a promotional website created by Twentieth Century Fox to explain what happened between the events of the original and the sequel.

As these events don't happen on-screen, I'm going to take what's written here loosely for the purposes of this book.

Though the website is now long defunct, the details have been lovingly retained on a *Wiki fandom* website. [015]

The details are sparse, but a spreadsheet lists the world cities destroyed in the three days over which the original film's events occurred. For the UK & ROI it lists the following:

- First wave: London.
- Second wave: Birmingham
- Third wave: Liverpool
- Intercepted wave: Belfast

Except for Belfast, instead of Dublin, this order of invasion closely ties in with my British and Irish invasion theory.

The website also states that only London, Birmingham and Liverpool were destroyed. This slightly differs from my theory, as the destruction would have surely involved more cities in between.

For example, Manchester isn't mentioned anywhere in this list, which I find strange.

I don't know if this was down to space on the website or just lack of detail in general, but as mentioned earlier, the information here is all taken with a pinch of salt.

What can be agreed, though, are the events of the global fightback in the film. A battle would occur probably somewhere over the Irish Sea, where our forces would intercept the City Destroyer.

The planned alien attack would be stopped in its path, with most of Ireland, Northern Ireland, Wales and Scotland escaping further devastation. For much of England, however, it would be a different story.

Scenario

The following worst-case scenario is predicted from events in the film. As none of the following events were depicted on-screen, logic and rough estimations are applied throughout.

1 On 2nd July 1996, as in other cities worldwide, a huge 15-mile wide 'City Destroyer' spaceship would appear over central London.

2 The Destroyer would hover over the capital for around six hours, before inevitably launching its simultaneous global surprise attack. A laser would shoot down onto Big Ben, creating a wall of fire to spread out from its epicentre across the city.

This wall of fire would engulf central London, laying waste to countless buildings and killing thousands. Anyone fortunate enough to be on the Underground during the attack would have a greater chance of survival.

3 The City Destroyer would proceed to its next target: Birmingham. As it heads north, the Destroyer would gyrate around the border of the M25 and take out as many satellite towns and suburbs along the way.

4 The City Destroyer would next follow the M40, attacking evacuees stuck in their cars. Reading and Oxford would be obliterated on the way. At this point there would be a drop in civilian casualties.

5 The aliens would eventually lose their element of surprise. Populations from most major cities would have long evacuated to the countryside, mountains or coastline.

6 There would be a counterstrike by the UK Armed Forces. Strategic positions such as Plymouth, Portsmouth, RAF Lakenheath, Chequers, Sandringham, Balmoral and Holyrood would all be taken out.

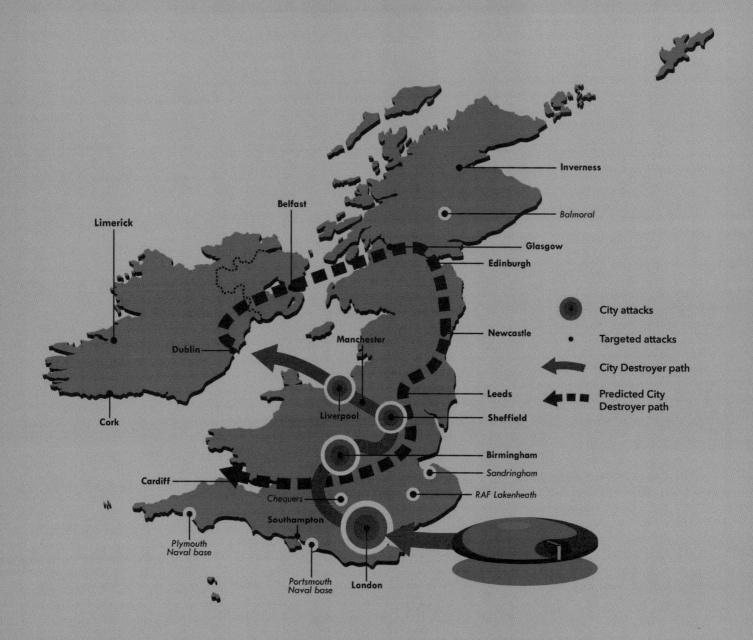

7 By the time the aliens arrived over Birmingham, the city would have long emptied. It would still be destroyed though, with the aliens taking out integral transport and supply infrastructures.

8 The Destroyer would next attack Wolverhampton, Derby, Nottingham and Sheffield, before moving across the Pennines to destroy Manchester and Liverpool.

9 The next target would be Dublin. It's at this point where the events of the film catch-up and lead to a successful global counter strike.

The City Destroyer would be taken down midway across the Irish sea. Northern Ireland, Scotland, northeast England and beyond would all be spared.

Survival outlook

It's not looking good for anyone in England to be honest. Key cities including London, Birmingham, Sheffield, Manchester and Liverpool all look set to bite the dust!

Any survivors in the southwest, far north or northeast of England will be counting their blessings. Everyone else across the Irish Sea and the other home nations will rejoice that they didn't get a close encounter. Without sounding too political, the wording of 'Independence Day' might also take on a whole new meaning due to England and its capital's weakened state.

The only thing that can unite us is the potential of an additional yearly Bank Holiday every 4th of July, where we too can celebrate with hotdogs and cigars just like our American cousins.

"This is not a war any more than there's a war between men and maggots." 016

WAR OF THE WORLDS

(2005) Dir: Steven Spielberg

I f you ever venture down the shadowy yet rather mundane back streets of Woking, you'll be in for a huge surprise. No, it's not a certain member of the Royal family dining at Pizza Express. This is something entirely different. Located in between a British Heart Foundation and Games Workshop marks the beginning of an alien invasion!

Rising high above street level and straddling several traffic bollards stands a 23-foot-high metallic alien tripod. You would have thought the invaders would have picked a more grandiose location like Washington D.C. or London to start their bid for global domination, instead of a sleepy commuter town in Surrey.

Of course, it's not real. Though the existence of non-humans in Woking might still be a question worth asking *(#jokes)*. The towering tripod was part of an art installation by sculptor Michael Condron. The piece celebrates the life and works of the celebrated science fiction author HG Wells, a former resident of the town.

Unveiled in a 1998 opening ceremony by no less than TV's Carol Vorderman, this metallic sculpture marks the landing spot of Martian invaders in the classic novel *War of the Worlds*. It's hardly blowing up the White House, but this imposing sculpture is a true testament to the legacy of HG Wells.

Alongside fellow author Jules Verne, Wells is considered one of the godfathers of science fiction.

You would have thought the invaders would have picked a more grandiose location

The celebrated author of *The Time Machine* and *The Invisible Man* was much ahead of his time, writing about worlds and technology that Victorian society had never envisaged before.

Wells wrote his novel as a response to the late 1800s British colonisation of the world. He considered the ultimate question: what if they were no longer top of the food chain? What if someone else came along more technologically advanced and treated the British with even more contempt than they did their own colonies?

In the seventy-five years since the author's death, Wells' cautionary tale has become the definitive alien invasion story and has lived on long in the public's consciousness. It has been adapted numerous times including Orson Welles' infamous 1938 radio play, George Pal's 1953 B-movie classic and Jeff Wayne's 1978 prog- rock spectacular.

The work of Wells would collide with another cinematic force in 2005, when iconic director Steven Spielberg adapted a new cinematic version of *War of the Worlds*.

Spielberg's previous extra-terrestrial experiences until this point had been rather more benign affairs, with both *Close Encounters of the Third Kind* (1977) and *E.T.* (1981) depicting more peaceful alien visitors. In these stories, the aliens communicated harmoniously with five musical notes or just wanted to make a phone call home.

War of the Worlds marked a sea change in the director's work. Known for his sense of wonderment and sentimentality, Spielberg had been on a much darker path since the mid-'90s. After directing the very personal and harrowing *Schindler's List* (1993), you wouldn't blame Spielberg for changing his style of direction.

In a period, that I call 'Spielberg Noir', the director took on more realistic, mature or grounded films. Just take a look at *Jurassic Park: The Lost World* (1997), *Amistad* (1997), *Saving Private Ryan* (1998), *A.I.* (2001) or *Minority Report* (2002) for example.

The marriage of Wells' nightmarish tale with Spielberg's new vision and some cutting-edge special effects were the perfect combination required to update *War of the Worlds* for a modern cinema audience. Spielberg's version is a disaster film on the grandest scale about society's collapse and survival. The film also echoed the public's paranoia and fear of terrorism, especially in the wake of the 9/11 attacks.

At the centre of the story was a realistic and personal perspective of life at the end of the world. For such an action-packed summer blockbuster and a Tom Cruise film to boot, it's a grim and nightmarish tale.

The film was, of course, a box office smash, but after repeat viewings, it leaves you with a bitter aftertaste and sense of helplessness. Despite being helmed by the usually heroic Tom Cruise, here he plays an entirely off-type character and is definitely no saviour! The heroics are downplayed.

Unlike *Independence Day* (1996), there is no wise-cracking Will Smith or hokey computer virus to bring down the mothership this time around. We're instead left to fend for ourselves in a cruel world and under the most extraordinary circumstances.

"Nice Planet! We'll take it!"

The film takes place over one weekend in modern-day Bayonne, New Jersey. We follow inept divorced dad, Ray Ferrier (Tom Cruise), as he reluctantly agrees to look after his two children, rebellious teenager Robbie (Justin Chatwin) and his younger sister Rachel (Dakota Fanning).

Things start in a mundane fashion, but trust this to be the weekend when there's a ruddy alien invasion! The film kicks off as news channels report several bizarre electrical storms raging across the world. In Ukraine, it's reported that all cities have suffered major power-cuts (00:07:59).

Another violent storm unexpectedly forms over New Jersey. Several large lightning bolts repeatedly strike the same location in the town (00:12:59).

An EMP (Electromagnetic Pulse; **see GoldenEye, pages 19-28**) immediately shuts down all power, causing phones and electrical devices to cease working. Every vehicle in the surrounding area grinds to a halt (00:16:48).

As the storm clears, Ray and several other townsfolk gather around a small impact crater. As more curious residents crowd around, the Earth violently shakes and gives away below (00:20:00).

Unearthly noises bellow out across the town as a huge 150-foot-high Tripod rises out of the crater. As the machine slowly cranks to life, the crowds gasp in amazement. Their excitement soon turns to terror as the Tripod attacks (00:24:00).

Hundreds are killed as the Tripod aimlessly fires laser beams into the screaming crowds below. People are disintegrated into piles of dust, leaving nothing but their clothes behind. Buildings explode, whilst cars are picked up and thrown around like toys.

A desperate Ray immediately runs back home and attempts to steal the only working car from a mechanic friend nearby. He drives away with his kids on board just as the street behind is destroyed in a massive explosion (00:29:30).

Cue lots of unnecessary screaming by Dakota Fanning's Rachel; a velociraptor standing on a Lego brick would sound less shrill. The rest of the film follows the Ferriers as they attempt to journey across-country to reunite with Ray's ex-wife at her parents' house in Boston.

'Take cover!' - A Japanese inspired flyer on how to hide from the Martian invaders.

Along the way, they survive a jumbo jet crash (00:37:25) and have their car stolen at gunpoint (00:49:14).

We also get some convenient plot explanation when Ray bumps into a scavenging TV news team. A news producer (Camillia Monet) acts as one of the film's primary sources of exposition.

In the news van, she relays footage to Ray and explains several key facts learnt from the invaders. First, unknown to Ray, there are many more Tripods attacking major cities all over the world. She plays a video showing several machines destroying an undisclosed city (00:42:07).

In further footage, one of the lightning strikes is slowed down. She explains that the aliens first arrived in vessels via lightning; the machines had probably been buried underground for a very long time (00:42:40).

A few hours pass as Ray and his family prepare to cross the Hudson River. Their passenger ferry however falls victim to a surprise Tripod attack (01:05:00). The aliens have now changed tactic; instead of disintegrating their victims on the spot, they now abduct and scoop up any straggling survivors.

As the boat capsizes, the Ferriers manage to swim ashore. Here they witness a full-on, yet futile, counter-assault by the US Military; where the Tripods are protected by impenetrable forcefields.

In the midst of the battlefield, the annoyingly petulant Robbie breaks free from Ray to go fight with the Army. As he disappears over a hill a huge explosion erupts as a Tripod

Unfortunately, there are no Welsh crooners at the end of War of the Worlds!

appears (01:07:29). With Robbie feared dead, Ray and Rachel reluctantly take cover in the basement of a nearby farmhouse with fellow survivor Harlan (Tim Robbins). As the three lay low, they discover that the aliens have stepped up their activity outside.

The invaders have started to cultivate a strange red-coloured vegetation, terraforming the land. It's revealed that the vegetation is made of human blood (01:15:43).

As hours turn to days, the three manage to avoid detection from the invaders outside. There are a couple of close calls, one in front of a serpent-like probe (01:17:30) and another with two marauding aliens (01:21:38).

An increasingly unhinged Harlan snaps and suffers a mental breakdown. Fearing his shouting will alert the aliens outside, Ray fights him in a restrained struggle, eventually leading to Harlan's death (01:28:04).

After several more hours of staying hidden, a returning probe discovers a sleeping Ray and Rachel (01:30:34). Ray attacks the probe with an axe while Rachel flees outside. Despite their fight, they are both abducted by a Tripod and placed in exterior hanging cages with several other abductees.

With the aid of a soldier's discarded grenade belt, Ray manages to blow up the Tripod from the inside. The wreckage falls to the ground as it explodes, freeing the abductees from their cages (01:35:00).

By the time *War of the Worlds* reaches its climax, the film unravels and loses some of its pace, as the story sticks closely to Well's original low-key, if slightly abrupt ending.

Ray and Rachel reach Boston, where collapsed Tripods are strewn across the city (01:37:00). We discover that the peculiar red alien vegetation is dying out too. The aliens have been beaten it seems by their deadliest of foes, bacteria! I know right?! A bit dull!

Bacteria. It's hardly the most thrilling cinematic conclusion. Perhaps the invading aliens were some kind of hyper-space-hygiene obsessives, and us Earthlings were just far too dirty for them?

Ray and Rachel arrive at his ex's parents' house in a surprisingly destruction-free part of the city. Amazingly, everyone in the house has survived the invasion intact, including an unscathed Robbie, who sneaks in for a father-son hug at the end (01:43:30).

This surprising ultra-happy ending harks to the end of the much sillier invasion film *Mars Attacks* (1996), which starred another famous Tom, Tom Jones of course. In the film Tom emerges from a remote desert cave after surviving a similar alien invasion.

He is greeted by several woodland creatures, with all the panache of a Disney princess. He then swings his hips in time to his hit song *It's Not Unusual* as it's played out over the credits.

Unfortunately, there are no Welsh crooners at the end of *War of the Worlds*! Its rather schmaltzy ending however quickly turns sour.

Just as the film cuts to black, Morgan Freeman's wise dulcet tones provide a serious proclamation on the fate of the rest of the world (01:44:00):

> *"From the moment the invaders arrived, breathed our air, ate and drank, they were doomed. They were undone, destroyed, after all of man's weapons and devices had failed, by the tiniest creatures that God in his wisdom put upon this Earth.*
>
> *By the toll of a billion deaths, man had earned his immunity, his right to survive among this planet's infinite organisms."*

One billion deaths! That figure is chilling! If you put that against Earth's 2005 population of 6.513 billion, that's just over 15% of the human race wiped out!

This, of course, makes you wonder what the circumstances would be for those in the UK. Would we suffer the same fate? Could we persevere? Or would we stand a better chance of survival if we stopped washing our hands after going to the toilet?

"Mars Attacks"

Hand hygiene aside, this wouldn't make a dent against the Martian occupiers, as the invasion would be relentless. As *War of the Worlds* only depicts events within the USA, the following theories and predictions are based on events that occur during the film. Applying the 15% death toll from Morgan Freeman's dulcet epilogue to the 2005 UK population of 60.18 million, rough estimations mean that nearly 10 million lives could be lost!

This is a staggering amount of people and clearly shows that the aliens mean business. Unlike in *Independence Day* (1996), where major cities are attacked one at a time over numerous days, here the rapid Tripod attacks could happen in any conceivable location.

From Cardiff to Cleethorpes or Norwich to Northwich, *War of the Worlds* would be hands-down the deadliest film in this book. Though the total number of Tripods attacking these shores would be up for speculation, we can roughly predict the Tripod numbers by reviewing key parts of the film.

The first one is seen when it attacks Bayonne, New Jersey (00:24:00). Later, during the news van scene, between ten and twelve Tripods are recorded attacking an unmentioned city (00:42:07). Finally, during the Hudson River crossing scene, nine Tripods can be counted (01:05:00).

There is roughly the same concentration of Tripods attacking the countryside as the cities. A rule of thumb considering the UK's compact geography would indicate you'd never be more than 10-15 miles away from bumping into a Tripod. This means that there could be easily between 300 and 400 Tripods stomping across the country.

In comparison, that's nearly the same number of Waitrose supermarkets* there are across the UK. Pray you don't get one of these in your area! (Tripods, that is! Stockists of 'Essential Flageolet Beans' and 'Essential Rosemary and sea salt Focaccia' are more than welcome.)

If you lived in a more urban city environment, the likelihood of multiple Tripod attacks would vastly increase. There would be no let-up for survivors, as the ferocity of each attack would not diminish.

If you lived in the countryside or in remote mountainous regions, then the chances of tripping over a set of metal tentacles would be reduced. However, that's not to say that you'd always be secure. According to the film, the alien's strategy appears to be to rapidly move from area to area, tactically herding and channelling survivors while attacking in increasingly larger formations.

So, it's anticipated that sooner or later, groups of Tripods would undoubtedly show up in your town. The opening narration sticks to HG Wells' words exactly, where we get some vague justification for the aliens' plans. Here Morgan Freeman lusciously declares:

> *"Yet across the gulf of space, intellects vast and cool and unsympathetic regarded our planet with envious eyes and slowly, and surely, drew their plans against us"* (00:02:06).

I'm not sure about you, but if I was jealous of a particular area, one that had great restaurants and pubs, with decent transport links or maybe a John Lewis nearby, I'd aspire to move there, not to blow it up! Must be a Martian thing.

If you were so unfortunate to be cornered by a Tripod, then you have two choices of death: 'Toast', where you are fired upon by lasers and disintegrated to ash in an instant (00:25:19) or 'Vegetation', a much grimmer demise, where you are abducted and scooped into the back of a Tripod and churned up into strange red plant material (01:35:00).

Both grisly demises however strangely involve the quick removal of a victim's clothes (00:25:35). Perhaps the aliens were really just aggressive second-hand clothing hunters?! That Tripod sculpture in Woking was erected next to a British Heart Foundation after all! Another major source of destruction occurs even before the Tripods appear: the use of EMPs (Electromagnetic Pulses). This is lightly touched on at the film's start when the town's power supply is shut down. Cars stop working, while mobile phones fall silent (00:16:48).

The fallout from an EMP attack would be a lot deadlier. In reality, the destruction from an EMP could cause a whole range of problems ranging from failing pacemakers all the way to planes dropping out of the sky **(see *GoldenEye*, pages 19–28)**.

So, in all you've roughly an 84% chance of survival, but if you're looking to keep it that way, then you'd have to stay alert and keep moving. Staying put in the same location for long periods of time would put you at risk of being discovered.

The best way of not being turned into Martian plant food is to stay silent, find shelter and keep one step ahead at all times. Geographically, anyone in the countryside or remote regions of the UK would stand a better chance of survival. Just don't rest on your laurels. Stay adaptive, and be ready to move in an instant. A major flaw I've noticed since reviewing the film is that before any attack, the Tripods blast out a low sounding horn (00:56:58).

One thing's for sure, it's really loud! So loud, in fact, that they give away their position. If you heard this, you'd hopefully have time to take shelter and hide.

Another way of avoiding the Tripods would be to sail offshore. However, this would all depend on the depth of the water around you, as the Tripods aren't exactly afraid of getting their tentacles wet (00:01:28).

The only solace to this whole invasion is it would only last for around a week or so. As quickly as it began, it would be over, as the Martians succumb to the deadly bacteria.

An additional source of contention to watch out for doesn't come from the aliens, but from other human survivors. During the invasion, civilisation would be pushed to the brink of collapse. With no food, no power and no utilities, society would fall into a lawless abyss.

If you were found to have the only working car or internet connection, you'd become the envy of everyone in town. Consider the scene when an angry mob steals Ray's car at gunpoint! ...replace that with a twelve-pack of toilet roll and now you're asking for trouble!

*349 Waitrose stores (2020)

Scenario

The following worst-case scenario is predicted from events in the film. As none of the following events were depicted on-screen, logic and rough estimations are applied throughout.

1 Several strange, powerful electrical storms would soon loom over much of the British Isles. Hundreds of lightning bolts would repeatedly strike up to an estimated 400 locations across the UK.

2 The alien invaders would secretly be transported to their Tripods through the lightning strikes, buried deep underground.

3 The electrical storms would generate EMPs (Electromagnetic Pulses). This would turn power grids off and render cars and electrical devices useless.

4 Within minutes, the Tripods would break through the surface and begin their attack. Towns and cities would be destroyed in quick succession. Anyone in their path would be obliterated to ashes by their lasers.

5 In larger metropolitan areas, groups of Tripods would eventually team up and attack in formation. People in the countryside and remote rural locations would fare best, however, this would be no guarantee of remaining 'Tripod free'.

6 The military would counter attack against the Tripods. Their strikes would however fail to dent the invaders. The Tripods' defences would be protected by forcefields.

7 After the initial attacks, nearly 48 hours into the invasion the aliens would change tactic. Any fleeing humans would run the risk of being rounded-up and abducted. If taken, survivors would be mashed-up and turned into Martian vegetation.

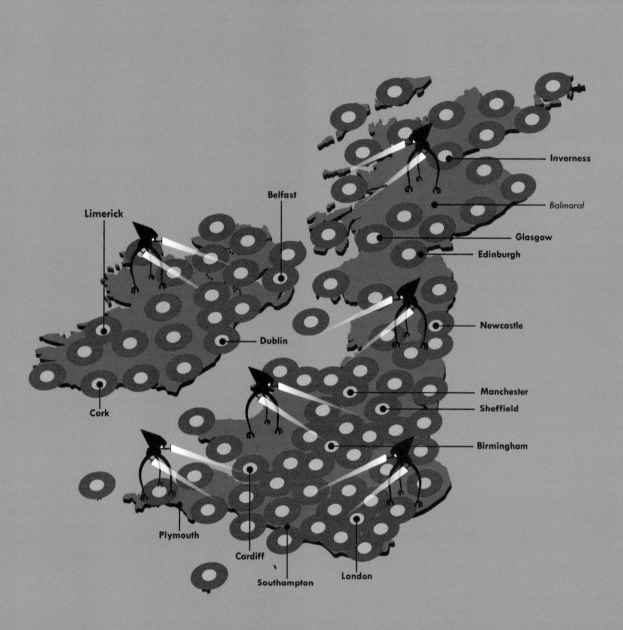

8 Any survivors taking shelter for long periods of time would run the risk of being tracked by the alien's serpent-like probes.

9 After one week, the aliens would succumb to deadly bacteria and start to die out. All Tripods will stop working and collapse. Any remaining aliens would turn to ash.

Survival outlook

Anyone in the countryside would stand a much better chance of survival, however the aliens' invasion plans would be so rapid and intense that anywhere in the UK could become a target. With up to 400 Tripods stomping across the nation, it could be only a matter of time before you eventually bumped into one of them.

Essentially, anyone could survive the invasion if they stayed hidden, silent and adapted to the Tripods' movements.

The major upside is it all only seems to last for one week. If you could make it through to the point where the Martians look a bit clammy or their Tripods begin to trip over themselves, then you'll know you've made it in one piece!

"They always go for
the landmarks!" [017]

INDEPENDENCE DAY: RESURGENCE

(2016) Dir: Roland Emmerich

As Bruce Willis' character John McClane says in *Die Hard 2 (1990), "How can the same shit happen to the same guy twice?"*

These immortal lines have become one of the main driving questions pursued by Hollywood in recent years, as each studio looks to expand any successful film, with high hopes of producing a money- spinning sequel, or better still creating a long running franchise. Just look at *Star Wars*, *James Bond*, *Marvel* or the *Fast and the Furious* series. All these properties started from humble origins to become the box office behemoths they are today.

The path to 'sequel-dom' though is a long and treacherous one. For every success like *Aliens* (1986), *The Bourne Supremacy* (2004) or *Jurassic World* (2015), you're just as likely to come across stinkers like *Jaws 2* (1978), *Speed 2* (1997) or *Crocodile Dundee in Los Angeles* (2001).

It's not like these films were designed to be awful. It's just that the originals were so good in the first place. How could they even compare? These sequels were ultimately left with limited options on where to expand their stories and desperately tried to look as if they weren't repeating themselves.

For example, Crocodile Dundee travels to another city, whilst Sandra Bullock curiously swaps a high-octane bus ride for a rather pedestrian and relaxing Caribbean cruise.

In *Jaws 2*, a hungrier shark takes over the carnage and ups the ante by actively hunting down Chief Brody's (Roy Scheider) children, in some kind of weird shark revenge mission; "Death Fish," as it were. Along the way, the shark develops an appetite for small floating rescue helicopters too!

Sloppy sequels have the power to turn people off an entire franchise. It can also put the original in disrepute. A lousy sequel doesn't need to be a rushed job either; some can be stuck in development hell for years. Decades can be taken to decide how to create a successful follow-up, with some of the best laid plans involving scripts, actors and budgets all falling at the wayside.

With the exception of the excellent *Mad Max: Fury Road* (2015) **(pages 131–140)**, the usual yard-stick adage of any sequel is the longer the gap from the original, the worse the film.

This overdrawn process can create problems with their intended fanbase too. Sequels that have taken decades to develop might have diminished over time. Whole generations of audiences who missed the cultural impact of an original film will no doubt misunderstand the significance of the sequel.

'Sky-high premium' - A mock-up insurance advert. Falling landmark cover is essential.

The phrase "Just because you can, doesn't mean you should" highlights the predicament of the 2016 sequel *Independence Day: Resurgence*, which arrived in cinemas more than twenty years after the success of its 1996 original.

As you can guess, I was a huge fan of *Independence Day*, so when I heard about the upcoming sequel, I was elated. Bigger spaceships! Advanced special effects! And even more Jeff Goldblum!

Unfortunately, the excitement turned to dread when the first set of reviews came out. Needless to say, my hopes had been dashed by the time I walked out of the cinema. *Resurgence* was a total mess and a crushing disappointment.

The plot was over-convoluted and featured too many new poorly conceived characters. It's an integral part of any disaster film to empathise with its characters, however here you become resigned to the fact that you simply don't care about any of them!

The spectacle disaster scenes, which had once been the series' calling card, felt largely flat and unexciting too. It's unfair to blindly judge *Resurgence* as just another poorly conceived sequel, however the original script and concept were drastically altered during early development, after leading star Will Smith dropped out.

The film bombed at the box office, taking only $389 million on a budget of $165 million. In comparison, the original took $817 million on almost half that budget.

Speaking to Yahoo News [018] in 2019, director Roland Emmerich spoke of his disappointment:

> *"I just wanted to make a movie exactly like the first, but then in the middle of production Will [Smith] opted out because he wanted to do Suicide Squad. I should have stopped making the movie because we had a much better script. After, I had to really fast, cobble another script together. And I should have just said 'no,' because all of a sudden I was making something I criticised myself, a sequel."*

It goes to show that having the best intentions for a film can change in an instant. The blame for the finished output of *Resurgence* however can't be fully placed at Will Smith's door, but it does make you wonder how the film would have panned out if he had stayed on.

The main problem the film faces is trying to escape the long shadow cast by its iconic original. They blew up the White House, for god's sake! How on Earth can you top that?

Emmerich even makes fun of this when he shows the White House inches away from destruction, just as one of the legs from the film's gigantic spaceships stops in front of the building (00:45:24).

Like all bad films, there's no way that a poorly prepared sequel can ever really touch its original. It's a tall order, especially when there's nowhere new or exciting to go.

Time might be kinder to *Resurgence* in the future, however, just like that rubbery shark eating that helicopter in *Jaws 2*, there's only one thing that a dreadful sequel like this can do to endure and live on; That's to fully embrace and celebrate in its own levels naffness and absurdity. And this film truly cranks up the levels of absurdity to the maximum setting!

Mothership happens

Resurgence takes place twenty years after the events of the original, in an alternative 2016. Society has fully embraced the leftover technology from the previous alien invasion, and everyone has become considerably more advanced.

Remember the late noughties, when anyone with an iPhone was incredibly annoying, pretending to drink beers on their phones, etc? That's exactly like everyone in this alternate universe, except here they have flying cars (00:03:00).

What the world doesn't realise is that aliens are on their way back! And this time, they're determined to have their revenge. In the original, the aliens had 15-mile-wide City Destroyers scattered across the globe and one giant orbiting mothership.

This time the aliens have changed tack and brought out the 'big guns' with one giant 3,000-mile-wide spaceship known as 'the Harvester'. Their new plan is to extract the Earth's molten core and destroy the planet.

The Harvester begins its path of destruction by entering the Earth's atmosphere above China and southeast Asia. It soon becomes apparent to anyone beneath the ship's path that it

has its own field of gravity. As it descends, skyscrapers are torn upwards. Boats, planes, cars and people all begin to float up into the air (00:39:00). As the foreboding ship continues to move across the globe, we next see it above London.

It's at this point the fields of gravity around the ship start to diminish. As Jeff Goldblum's character remarks, "What comes up must come down". On-screen, everything floating in the sky east of Shanghai is suddenly dropped onto the streets of London.

The film has its profound "shark eating a helicopter" moment when the Burj Khalifa smashes down in front of the London Eye (00:41:00). Seconds later, the levels of absurdity are cranked up again, when another well-known landmark, Malaysia's Petronas Towers, smacks down on top of Tower Bridge (00:41:50).

The distance between the Burj Khalifa and the Petronas Towers is over 3,400 miles. For them to float merrily in the sky together for a further 3,400 miles and land nearly 2 miles apart in central London is just ridiculous.

The Harvester crosses the Atlantic, where it begins to settle. Several giant 300-mile-long fold-down legs then descend outwards from all sides of the ship. They scrape across whatever land or water is in front of them before coming to a halt. As the legs descend, they destroy countless cities and kill thousands (00:44:02). In oceans, they create huge localised tsunamis that rise up and crash against coastlines (00:45:00).

It's hard to contemplate the ship's scale, but there are a couple of scenes where you can see part of the ship set against the Florida panhandle. It's vast, straddling the entire Atlantic Ocean (01:04:50).

With the Harvester in position, it beams down a laser into the middle of the Atlantic to slowly extract the Earth's molten core (00:51:40). Just like in the original, the Armed Forces retaliate, but once again, they fail miserably. There's also more plot involving a friendlier alien race with what I can only describe as a very large 'Persil ball'.

A plan is hatched to stop the Harvester and take out the very large alien queen residing inside. Of course, the Americans win and kill the queen, which causes the Harvester ship to take off and leave (00:58:04).

In the end, there isn't even a big explosive payoff (probably a good thing with the ship still over the Atlantic). There aren't even cigars, hotdogs or fireworks to celebrate like in the original. Overall, it's just not as much fun.

One positive is that it truly feels like an international experience, with a varied supporting cast of different nationalities. The apocalyptic levels of destruction aren't just reserved for the US either. In a slightly strange morbid way, it's refreshing to see London bite the dust on-screen for once, although just how many falling global landmarks were harmed in the process, I dread to think.

'Act of falling Burj Khalifa'

I'm not sure what type of insurance would cover you against "an act of falling Burj Khalifa"? The events in *Resurgence* are so outlandish that anything could happen.

In the same way as a child tipping their box of toys onto a carpet from high above, anyone below could fall victim to large objects (and landmarks) falling from out of the sky.

The only benefit to anyone in the British Isles and other parts of Europe would be that the levels of gravity here would remain normal.

This would mean anyone caught out in the open would still stand a good chance of survival by running or driving away, just as long as they looked up at the same time.

Another positive is that the duration of falling objects wouldn't last too long, however the damaging effects could still be catastrophic. It would be strongly advised to stay clear of anywhere incendiary like nuclear power stations, oil refineries or petrol stations, just to be on the safe side.

Looking at the designs of the Harvester and its position on-screen, we can roughly work out the path of its terrifying extractor legs.

Unfortunately, it will be a truly horrible day for anyone in the Republic of Ireland, South Wales or the West Country. If you drew a diagonal line from Galway down to Southampton, anyone west of that line would more than likely have the Earth move for them, whether they liked it or not.

Just pray that the aliens don't come back for a third time, because god knows how they'd even attempt to top any of this!

Scenario

The following worst-case scenario is predicted from events in the film. As only some of the following events were depicted on-screen, logic and rough estimations are applied throughout.

1 On 4th July 2016, the aliens would return and descend into the Earth's atmosphere in a giant 3,000-mile-wide spaceship (the Harvester). From China and East Asia, the flight path would journey west.

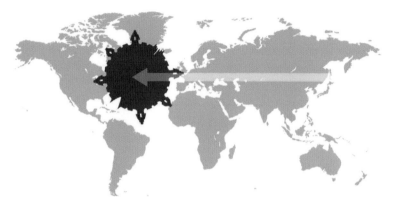

2 As the Harvester descends, it would initially develop its own field of gravity. This would cause anything on the surface to suddenly break free and lift upwards. Buildings, planes, boats, cars and people are lifted up into the air.

3 As the Harvester journeys westwards towards the Atlantic, the field of gravity surrounding the ship would slowly dissipate. Anything floating around the ship would suddenly drop without warning.

4 Over in the UK and Irish Republic, objects would rain down immediately. This would cause random destruction everywhere. Best avoid petrol stations, nuclear power stations and oil refineries.

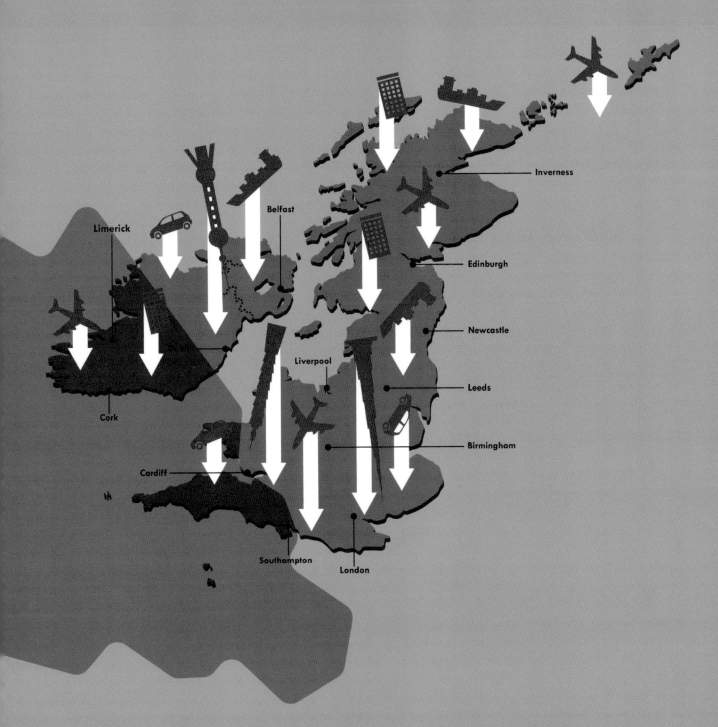

5 Anyone inside tunnels or using underground networks would be shielded from much of the destruction above.

6 The destruction would be over quickly, but the devastation and casualty rate would be catastrophic.

7 One of the Harvester's 300-mile-wide legs would cut a path across Ireland, South Wales and the West Country. Anyone in the way would be flattened. The leg would plough through any towns, coastal areas and countryside.

Survival outlook

It doesn't bode well for everyone in the UK to be honest. So, best look up before you leave the house that morning, as it could be raining cats and dogs and people... and cars, trains, buses, oil tankers, buildings, aeroplanes! Anything from above, with falling national landmarks reserved as the deadliest!

The best chance of survival would be to head to any caves, tunnels or underground networks. But you'd have to be quick, as just like any average downpour, it would be over before you knew it!

Anyone in Ireland, South Wales or the West Country would also face the double whammy of destruction from being in the path of one of the Harvester's 300-mile-wide landing legs.

That annual holiday to Butlin's Minehead is off. Permanently!

NATURE STRIKES BACK!

"So, this is it. If the
world does go on,
It will not go on for
everyone." [019]

DEEP IMPACT

(1998) Dir: Mimi Leder

After the commercial success of *Independence Day* (1996), the 'Disaster movie' would once again rule over Hollywood.

In the late '90s at the height of their popularity, rival studios would compete in head-to-head box office bouts with similar disaster movie properties.

The first major fight occurred in 1997, when Universal's *Dante's Peak* and Fox's *Volcano* tussled over which studio had the hottest lava-based catastrophe. Though both were mildly successful, *Dante's Peak* and *Volcano* received largely lukewarm responses from critics and audiences alike.

The next year, the destruction stakes would be raised even higher, when Disney and DreamWorks went toe-to-toe in 'The Battle of Asteroid v Comet'.

In the red corner was 'team asteroid': Disney's *Armageddon* (1998), a big, sweaty, brain-at-the door Bruce Willis and Jerry Bruckheimer vehicle.

Armageddon depicted the total destruction of Paris courtesy of an asteroid and a soundtrack featuring Aerosmith's wedding earworm, *"I don't want to miss a thing"*. Which of the two is the deadlier is up for discussion.

Whilst in the blue corner was 'team comet': DreamWorks' more cerebral *Deep Impact* (1998). This was a less fun, character-driven epic, that focused on the personal dramas and sacrifices involved during life at the end of the world. It also featured one of cinema's finest world leaders in Morgan Freeman's President Beck.

When the final bell rang, *Armageddon* was declared the victor, with a total global box office haul of $554m, compared to *Deep Impact's* $349m.

While *Armageddon* was undoubtedly the more popular film, *Deep Impact* has left a lasting impression over the years. Looking back now, it's the deadlier of both films by a landslide, or should I say mega-tsunami.

As mentioned in my prologue, *Deep Impact* has been burnt into my memory. But, more importantly, the film raised greater "what if" questions concerning the fate of the UK and the rest of the world.

Great job, astronauts!

In *Deep Impact*, the human race faces total annihilation from an 11-mile-long comet set on a collision course with Earth. A team of NASA astronauts led by Robert Duvall are sent to space several months before on a mission

Bridges and skyscrapers are twisted and torn apart like matchwood

to intercept and destroy the comet before it destroys us. Towards the end of the film, the brave astronauts inventively make the ultimate sacrifice and save the Earth by flying their explosively charged NASA spacecraft deep into the chasm of the comet.

They succeed and blow the comet to smithereens. However along the way, they make the odd mistake. Unfortunately that one odd mistake involves killing millions of people back on Earth.

During the mission's first detonation attempt, the astronauts massively bodge things up! Instead of blowing up the comet entirely, they make things a whole lot worse (and wetter) for everyone back home; the astronauts only manage to shear off part of the comet.

A smaller fragment, 1.5 miles in length, breaks off and strikes the Earth first. This section of comet plunges into the Atlantic Ocean, just off the coast of North Carolina. This causes a nightmarish mega-tsunami (1,400 ft. high) to rise up and plough into the eastern seaboard of the United States.

On-screen (care of some now-dated '90s CGI) the massive wave approaches the US coastline at the speed of sound (01:42:00).

The skyline of New York City is engulfed by the enormous wall of water. Bridges and skyscrapers are twisted and torn apart like matchwood. Even the poor old Statue of Liberty isn't spared as her head is decapitated and tossed around the streets of Manhattan like a discarded bath toy.

The horrific scenario continues as the wave heads further inland and wipes out many small towns and communities for hundreds of miles. The catastrophic death would be estimated at anywhere between 80 and 100 million people. Once again, nice job, astronauts!

Wellies required?

For those hoping that this disaster would be strictly a North American affair, you're sadly mistaken.

Towards the close of the film (01:50:00), Morgan Freeman gives a speech to a crowd of survivors in front of a partially rebuilt Capitol Building. Here he remarks that *"the wave hit the coastlines of Europe and Africa too"*.

Gulp! So, what does that mean for everyone in the UK? Would my insurance cover me? And more importantly, would I need wellies? We can come up with some basic theories about the wave from the doom-laden television broadcast that the President gives partway through the film (01:29:00):

"The smaller of the two comets will hit first; somewhere along the Atlantic seaboard, probably in the waters off the coast of Cape Hatteras, in just over 12 hours at 4:35 pm Eastern daylight time.

The comet is going to be, well… disastrous. There will be a very large tidal wave moving quickly through the Atlantic Ocean. It will be 100 feet high, travelling at 1,100 miles per hour, that's faster than the speed of sound.

As the wave reaches shallow water, it's going to slow down, but the wave height (depending on the shelf off the coast) will be 1,000 to 3,500 feet high. When the land is flat the wave will wash inland 600 to 700 miles.

The wave will hit our nation's capital 40 minutes after impact. New York City, Boston, Atlanta, Philadelphia; all will be destroyed. If you have any means of getting away from the path of this wave, leave now!"

The distance between Cape Hatteras and Land's End in Cornwall is roughly 3,400 miles. This means the wave could travel across the Atlantic in less than 4 hours!

The fact that the President's broadcast gave an initial warning of 12 hours means the population of the UK would have a total of 16 hours to get to safety. Speaking about similar asteroid strikes in a *Guardian* interview, [020] Duncan Steel from the University of Salford stated that:

"A wave would work in principle like a stone being thrown into a pond. The ripples would take seconds to spread to the banks.

The same effect would be applied here but on a grander scale."

The initial height of the wave on the European side would be considerably less than that of the US wave, due to the wave losing some of its initial energy as it travels across the ocean. It would however be no less deadly.

Based on the film's events, the wave that strikes New York City is taller than the Empire State Building, at around 1,400 ft. President Beck's speech reveals that the wave managed to reach the Ohio and Tennessee valleys, a distance of nearly 650 miles!

Rough workings out and the finest fag packet science estimate that our wave could be 500–600 ft, potentially more than twice the height of Big Ben! This could travel inland for around 200 to 300 miles!

Also, if you were expecting just one wave, that might be pure optimism, as an impact this size could create a series of large waves, due to water being displaced and leftover from the large vacuum caused by the impact.

According to the same *Guardian* article,[019] Dr Steven Ward from the Institute of Geophysics and Planetary Physics at the University of California believes:

"The greatest wave amplitude would be further back because the tsunami would continue to be boosted by the water oscillating up and down at the epicentre. To see what happens, over a much shorter time scale, drop a sugar cube into a cup of coffee."

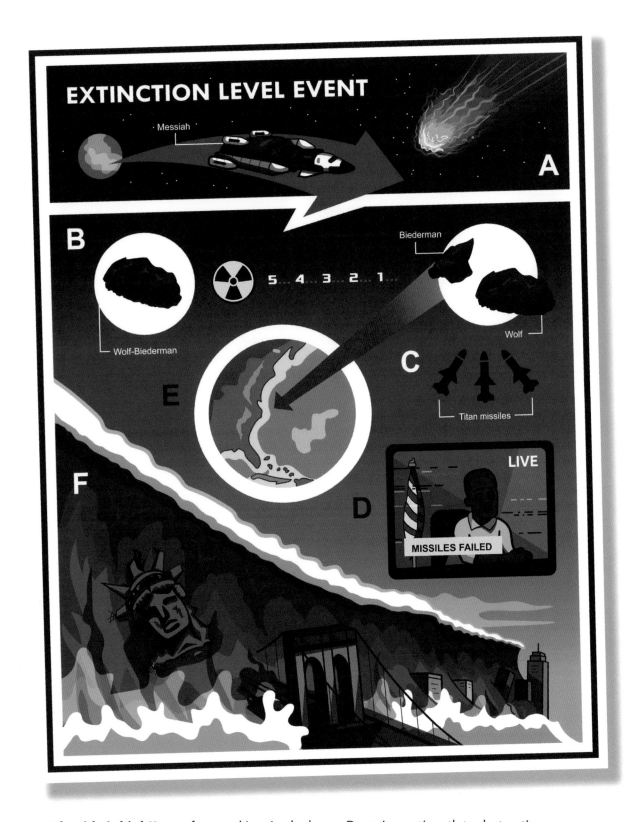

'**The tide is high!**' - a safety card inspired take-on *Deep Impact's* path to destruction.

Scenario

The following worst-case scenario is predicted from events in the film. As none of the following events were depicted on-screen, logic and rough estimations are applied throughout.

1   Between 8 and 10 pm BST, the first tsunami would approach the UK and Irish coastline. They would approach in a north-easterly direction and slow down as they gained height.

2   The height of the waves would be estimated at near-twice the size of Big Ben, around 500–600 ft. This would be disastrous. Large parts of the south coast of England would be engulfed. Key cities including Plymouth, Southampton, Portsmouth and Brighton would be completely wiped out.

3   The initial wave would continue to travel inland in a north-easterly direction at a devastating pace. Bristol, Cardiff, Gloucester and Oxford would all lie in its path.

4   Across the Irish Sea, the Irish Republic and Northern Ireland would take the brunt of the initial wave; cities including Cork, Limerick and Derry/Londonderry would be flattened on impact. The wave would continue to move across the countryside, taking out the capitals of Dublin and Belfast.

5   Back in England, as the wave roars inland, it would start to lose some of its initial height (300–500 ft.). It would reduce in speed, but would be no less devastating. London would be engulfed next, as well as miles of low-lying land along the southeast coast.

6   The wave would wrap around the sides of Welsh mountains and hit Birmingham. It would then sweep further north into the Manchester and Liverpool areas.

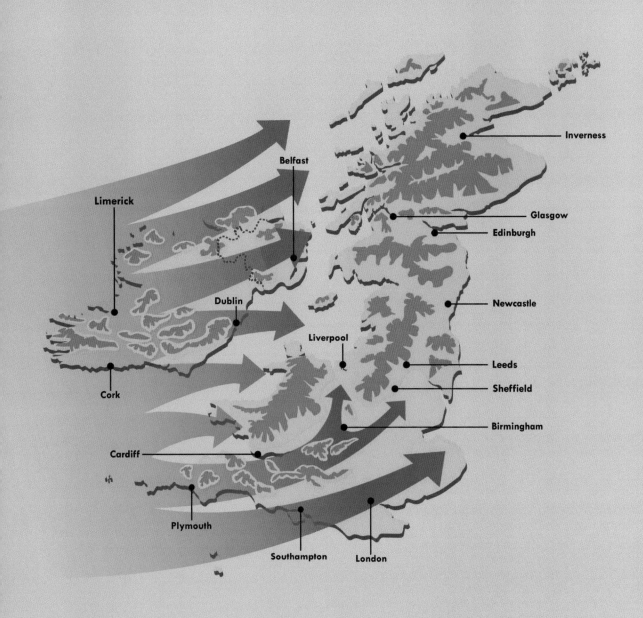

7 The Pennines would act as a barrier to the waves, preventing them from going any further north. Key cities, including Sheffield and Leeds, would sit smugly shielded.

8 The majority of Scotland would breathe easy. The brunt of the waves would instead be taken out by the Irish coastline. Any subsequent waves would crash into the Scottish Highlands and Islands.

9 The majority of the northeast coast stretching from Hull to Edinburgh would remain high and dry.

Survival outlook

If you live on the northeast coast of England or Scotland, then you'd be sitting high and dry. Unfortunately, that joint Newcastle stag and hen do you've been reluctantly forced to go on look's more than likely to be going ahead after all.

Everyone else in the Scottish Hebrides, across the Irish Sea, below the Pennines or to the east of the Welsh mountains, will need something more robust than a pair of wellies.

That said, everyone in the UK would still have a good head start of 16 hours to seek out some Kendal Mint Cake and plan their best Duke of Edinburgh climbs to get to 600ft above sea level or higher.

"Gentlemen, to England!"
"To mankind!"
"To Manchester United!" [021]

THE DAY AFTER TOMORROW

(2004) Dir: Roland Emmerich

f at first you fail to destroy the world. *Try and try again.*" This could easily be the mission statement of any Bond villain.

In this instance, it also applies to the cinematic force that is "The Master of Disaster", Director Roland Emmerich.

In the mid-'90s, after the success of sci-fi blockbusters *Universal Soldier* (1992), *Stargate* (1994) and *Independence Day* (1996), the German-born director, along with his producing partner Dean Devlin, could do no wrong.

However, all it took to end this box office streak was the fallout from one giant turkey, or in this case, a radioactive lizard! The 1998 version of *Godzilla* promised so much, but squandered every opportunity it had been presented.

Overall, the film came across as another cheap *Jurassic Park* knock-off, thinly layered behind another excuse to tear up New York.

Emmerich's remake was a massive disappointment that alienated fans of the Japanese original, whilst poor word of mouth kept audiences away.

Godzilla was by no means a major box office flop: the film still managed to take $379 million worldwide. But with a budget of nearly $150 million and an additional $80 million spent on marketing alone, meant there were very slim pickings left for Columbia Pictures executives to scrap over.

With one giant reptilian tail hung sheepishly between their legs, Emmerich and Devlin retreated from their usual world of high stakes sci-fi and began work on their next project. This time they took on another dastardly foe – the British, no less – in Mel Gibson's hiss and snarl American revolutionary epic, *The Patriot* (2000).

Finally, the world was safe from impending disaster, well, for now at least. *The Patriot* however marked the end of Emmerich and Devlin's near decade of producing films together.

After the split, Devlin would produce CGI spider B-movie *Eight Legged Freaks* (2002), whilst Emmerich would return to what he was best at: destroying the world one film at a time.

In his time away, however, the world had drastically changed. After the events of 9/11, the appetite for fast and loose disaster epics had waned.

It took some time for Emmerich to figure out what to do next and how to deliver to a far more conscientious and sensitive audience. Instead of searching the skies above for imminent disaster, for his next project he focused his attention on the Earth and tackled something far more pressing and topical.

Emmerich would take on climate change head-on in *The Day After Tomorrow* (2004). The tone was serious, but this film had all the panache and over-the-top relish that audiences had become accustomed to.

Speaking to *Collider.com* [022] in October 2019, Emmerich remarked:

> *"When you think about global warming, anything can happen with climate change. You might radically tell it, but the underlying science was totally real. So, I acquired the rights [to the book The Coming of the Global Superstorm] and changed the title and wrote it a bit in the style of Independence Day."*

For a film about the weather, bright and sunny skies don't exactly make for great drama, so each disaster is exaggerated and then some! Tornados, tsunamis and ice storms are all thrown at the screen with great abandon.

The Day After Tomorrow looked to shake audiences' cinema seats and rattle their recycling boxes at the same time

No monument is left unscathed as the planet is braced for impact! Behind the spectacle lay a more serious message; how much abuse can Mother Nature take before she inevitably snaps back?

Storm Warning!

For a 2004 release, *The Day After Tomorrow* was light years ahead in its attempts to tackle climate change. For context, the Paris climate accord was twelve years away from being signed, UK supermarkets were eleven years away from banning free plastic bags, whilst activist Greta Thunberg was one year old.

Attempts to create environmental blockbusters had previously been kicked into the long grass. *Waterworld* **(pages 120-133)** had tried in 1995, but with limited success.

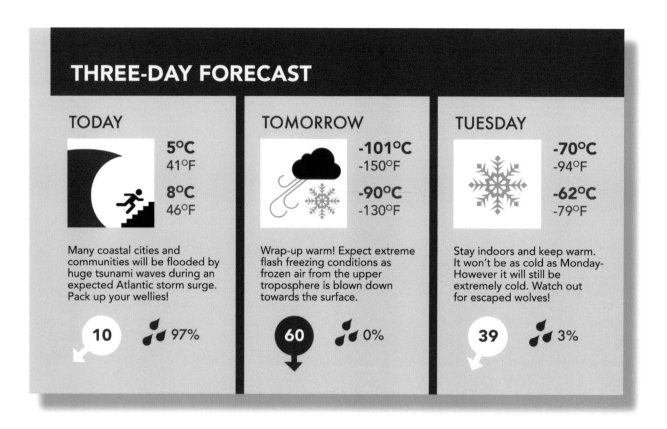

THREE-DAY FORECAST

TODAY

5°C
41°F

8°C
46°F

Many coastal cities and communities will be flooded by huge tsunami waves during an expected Atlantic storm surge. Pack up your wellies!

10 💧 97%

TOMORROW

-101°C
-150°F

-90°C
-130°F

Wrap-up warm! Expect extreme flash freezing conditions as frozen air from the upper troposphere is blown down towards the surface.

60 💧 0%

TUESDAY

-70°C
-94°F

-62°C
-79°F

Stay indoors and keep warm. It won't be as cold as Monday- However it will still be extremely cold. Watch out for escaped wolves!

39 💧 3%

'Foreboding Forecast !' - how *The Day After Tomorrow's* weather forecast might look in the paper.

The Day After Tomorrow looked to shake audiences' cinema seats and simultaneously rattle their recycling boxes.

The film follows rugged paleoclimatologist Jack Hall (Dennis Quaid) as he discovers to his horror that his rapid climate change theory has become a reality. The Atlantic Ocean current system known as the AMOC (Atlantic Meridional Overturning Circulation) has been disrupted by freshwater from melted polar ice caps.

The new ocean temperatures have thrown the northern hemisphere's weather systems into complete chaos and taken the planet to the brink of a new ice age! Jack's drastic attempts to warn the authorities are however ignored.

Cue some CGI climate craziness as giant hailstones pummel Tokyo (00:11:15), and multiple tornadoes destroy Los Angeles (00:26:00).

Meanwhile, the US eastern seaboard is hit by a 60-foot-high storm surge. Then, just like in *Deep Impact* **(pages 95-102)**, the Statue of Liberty takes another beating by a giant tsunami (00:48:10).

New York is completely engulfed and cut off from the rest of the world. But that soon becomes the least of everyone's problems, as three vast super storms form across the northern hemisphere and begin to plunge temperatures across the planet.

As the floodwaters freeze, the impending storms pose a new deadly threat: each storm eye, known as a vortex, has the power to drag freezing cold air (-150°F/-101°C) from the upper atmosphere. This deadly air can instantly freeze anything on impact!

Jack pleads for action from leaders during a national security briefing. He draws a line across a map of the USA that stretches from Washington D.C. to Southern California (01:04:00). He then pleads with the Vice President (Kenneth Welsh) to immediately start evacuations and get anyone living below that line as far south as they can.

Fearing the worst, Jack mounts a small rescue team to find his son Sam (Jake Gyllenhaal), who along with a small group of survivors, is stranded inside the New York Central Library.

Using skis and sledges, Jack and his colleagues Frank (Jay O. Sanders) and Jason (Dash Mihok) start navigating the hazardous frozen landscape and travel the 230 miles from Washington D.C. to New York.

Tragedy however soon strikes when Frank falls to his death through the glass roof of a shopping mall. As temperatures continue to fall, back in New York, disaster occurs when Sam's girlfriend, Laura (Emmy Rossum), becomes sick from a blood poisoning injury.

Now, in dire need of penicillin, Sam and his fellow survivors venture beyond the library in a desperate race against time to search for medical supplies. They eventually secure some penicillin, whilst a pack of dodgy CGI wolves add some unnecessary tension.

The real drama however unfolds high above the city, as the eye of a superstorm looms on the horizon.

Skyscraper windows shatter as deadly freezing cold air rapidly descends onto the streets below (01:39:20). Sam and his friends rush back to the library, where they clamber around a roaring fire and barricade themselves inside.

Simultaneously, on the outskirts of the city, Jack and an injured Jason frantically hack through the roof of a nearby restaurant, where they take shelter inside a kitchen.

As the storm passes, Jack and Jason make it to the library, reuniting with Sam and his fellow survivors (01:49:00). Jack later contacts US government officials, who relay helicopters to rescue the group and search for more survivors.

During the film's closing scenes, it's revealed that the world has changed beyond repair. The fallout from the climate shift has left the world in a topsy-turvy predicament.

The once poor southern developing countries have been left in a position of power, with the richer northern nations such as Canada and the USA succumbing to an inhospitable frozen tundra.

Ironically, the US president issues a humbled televised national address from the confines of the US embassy in Mexico (01:51:50).

In the film it's revealed that the Mexican government has agreed to open up the border to US citizens after negotiating with the US to wipe away all Latin American debt.

This particular flip in national dominance stays with you long after the film ends and acts as a cautionary tale. Running throughout, there's also a satirical commentary on George W. Bush's presidency and his 2004 environmental policies, especially regarding climate change and Alaskan oil exploration. Actor Kenneth Welsh even bears a striking resemblance to then US Vice President Dick Cheney.

The Day After Tomorrow means well in its earnest eco convictions. That's not to say that behind all the spectacular CGI nonsense lies a hollow experience. On the contrary, there might be some genuine scientific truth behind the film.

At *Business Insider.com*, [023] Francesco Muschitiello, the author of a 2018 study of the AMOC (Atlantic Meridional Overturning Circulation), revealed that the circulation of the Atlantic was currently in its most weakened state in over 1,600 years.

Despite this, Muschitiello added that any disruption in the ocean's water circulation would take over 400 years to make any impact on the climate, not the mere days it took to form a new ice age on-screen. So, the key question is, how would the UK fare?

I'll get my coat

Whereas Emmerich only destroyed US cities in *Independence Day*, here he opens the rest of the world to a good old rollicking. Luckily for the UK, we don't have to speculate on what happens, as some of the action takes place on these shores.

The UK's main cause of concern is an emerging superstorm. From the onset, it looks like we'd experience the same polar conditions as the US.

We see a precursor to the later events in New York when freezing cold air from the upper atmosphere is dragged over the Scottish Highlands. During one scene, three UK military helicopters fly towards the Balmoral estate to rescue the royal family. Disaster strikes as they pass through a storm vortex.

The sub-zero cold air from the upper atmosphere causes each helicopter to lose power and fall out of the sky. Evacuating crew members instantly freeze to death as they try to flee their craft (00:40:10). When I first viewed this in the cinema, I thought the helicopters already had the royal family onboard and were flying away from Balmoral.

I've always had visions of several Corgis turning into instant popsicles during this scene. Emmerich would later feature a look-alike of the Queen and her corgis (very much alive) cameoing in future disaster epic *2012* (2009).

We can see the position of the three superstorms AKA "cells" on Jack's computer screen (00:53:00). The first cell follows the events as played out in the film and is tracked through Canada and The United States.

The second European cell covers much of continental Europe, including the Nordics, the British Isles, and large parts of the continental mainland. Finally, the third, Asian cell, covers large swathes of Siberia, Japan, China and the Korean peninsula.

For our concern, the predicted path of the European storm, particularly the vortex, looks set to expand in size over Iceland and later the UK and France. It's not looking good for anyone in the UK, as there would be nowhere to hide from the storm.

The only way to stay safe would be to knuckle down and stay warm with plenty of food and supplies. There's a high likelihood that some utilities would be cut off. So, make sure that you find a place with plenty of fuel to burn. The New York survivors had the right frame of mind by holding up in the city's library.

Due to UK budget cuts, I'm not sure you'd be as lucky to find a library or one with so many books. So an alternative option is to head to your nearest charity shop where I'm sure you'd find an abundance of copies of *The Da Vinci Code*, released a year previously in 2003.

The most dangerous part of surviving "Frozen Tundra Britain" would be to stay sheltered as the vortex passes above. Once clear, it would be safer to venture out, but best keep an eye out for any hazards beneath the snow.

Anyone in Newcastle would in no doubt be testing the waters with as minimal clothing as possible. If it's too cold for Geordies, then what hope do we have?!

There's no mention of any of the other infrequent weather conditions featured in the film either, so there would probably be no tornadoes or giant hailstorms.

Prior to the storm surge striking New York, the US news reports that a wind-driven storm surge struck the Nova Scotia coast and was expected to hit the US and Canadian seaboard later that day (00:43:55). This storm surge isn't confirmed to hit the UK or any other country, but this can't be ruled out.

Towards the end of the film, we get a brief reveal of Europe from high above in the orbiting International Space Station (01:46:00). With much of the storm cleared, we can see the broader picture of the continent.

Anywhere beneath central Spain and Italy looks to have escaped much of the damage, whilst anywhere above looks set to be consumed by the new barren landscape of ice and snow.

The Nordics, France, Germany and Poland will be rendered inhospitable. The UK, it seems, will be smack bang in the centre of this new polar region. It will be difficult to evacuate any British survivors through France and Spain while avoiding the eye of the storm. Many people would, unfortunately, perish.

The only hope for British survivors might lie on the beaches of the Costa Blanca and other Mediterranean holiday resorts. Any Brits stuck in Benidorm for a week's holiday will no doubt probably emerge from their sun loungers, cocktail in hand, just wondering what all the fuss was about.

The British way of life will continue behind all those gold medallions, shop mobility scooters and sunburnt blisters. We will prevail… well, sort of.

Scenario

The following worst-case scenario is predicted from events in the film. As only some of the following events were depicted on-screen, logic and rough estimations are applied throughout.

1 The European superstorm cell would develop somewhere over the North Atlantic, near the Icelandic coast.

2 The cell would increase in size and drastically change weather patterns across the continent. The dropping temperatures would affect all of Northern Europe.

3 The eye of the storm would make landfall somewhere across the Scottish Highlands. Anyone close to the eye would fall victim to freezing temperatures of - 150°F/ - 101°C, as cold air is dragged from the upper atmosphere.

Three Military helicopters on a mission to rescue the royal family would fall out of the sky. The crews onboard will all freeze to death.

4 The UK will endure some of the worst blizzards in recorded history. The storm would move south across the rest of the British Isles; anyone exposed by the storm eye will experience dramatic freezing conditions and certain death.

5 The storm will gradually move southwards away from the UK. In its wake, it will leave a permanent icy and snowy tundra. The storm clouds would linger long after the weather patterns began to change.

6 One week on, any survivors could leave the safety of their shelters. The landscape would resemble a harsh polar environment. Anyone looking to survive in this new brutal landscape will need supplies, protection and fuel.

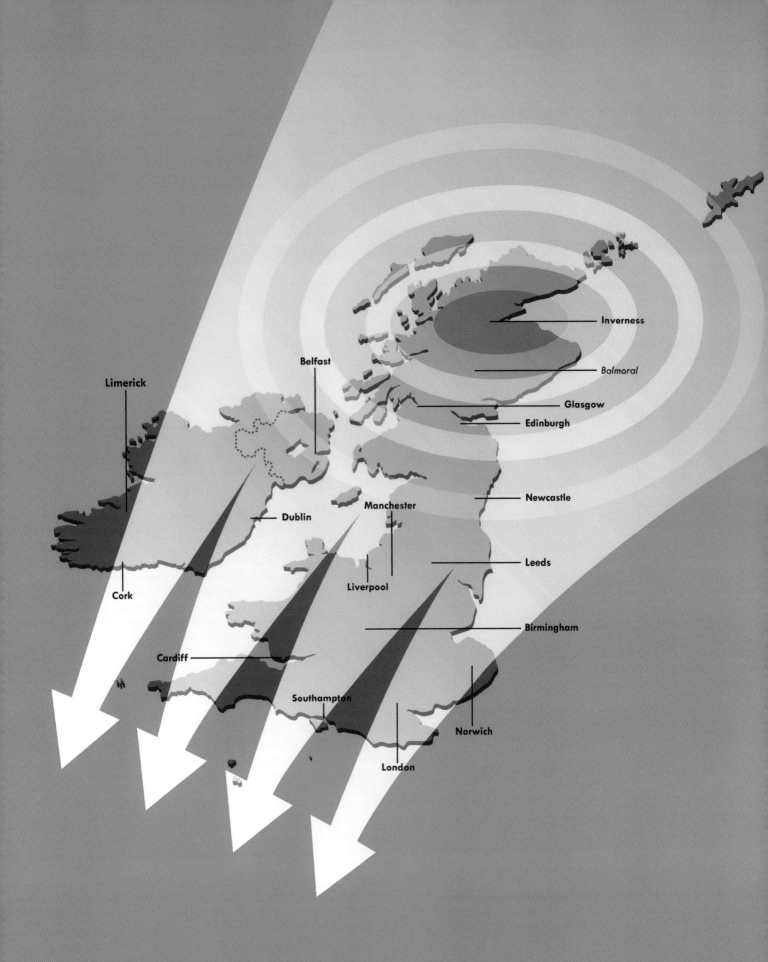

Limerick

Belfast

Inverness

Balmoral

Glasgow

Edinburgh

Dublin

Newcastle

Manchester

Liverpool

Leeds

Birmingham

Cardiff

Cork

Southampton

Norwich

London

Survival outlook

No location in the British Isles would avoid this rapid change in weather. The severe dip in temperatures brought on by the European superstorm would be cataclysmic. Only by travelling 1,000–15,000 miles south would anyone be able to completely escape the chaos.

The UK would be left under a permanent blanket of ice and snow. Chances of survival in this new polar apocalypse would be very slim indeed. Though it would still be possible, as long as you stayed inside and had enough fuel and food supplies to get through.

So, get your hot water bottle out and pop that kettle on – as you could be in this for the long haul!

BRAVE NEW WORLDS

"Dry land is not just
our destination;
it's our destiny!" ₀₂₄

WATERWORLD

(1995) Dir: Kevin Reynolds

don't know what it is about *Waterworld* (1995). This turbocharged yet choppy, mullet-riddled actioner is a film that I'm forever tempted by.

No matter how many times it's on ITV2, I'm always inclined to drop whatever I'm doing and sit down to watch.

Set on a post-apocalyptic Earth, after the polar ice caps have melted, *Waterworld* is pure captivating carnage. Perhaps my obsession with the film comes down to the fact that we were both deeply un-popular back in the 1990s.

After all, I was this spotty fat kid with a weird ginger side-parting going on – such a 'trendsetter'!

Being a proud outsider, I've always been drawn to things that others tend to dislike. I'm the guy who loves leftover toffee pennies from tins of Quality Street at Christmas. And dare I say it, prefers *Grease 2* (1982) over *Grease* (1978) any day of the week!

I lovingly embrace *Waterworld* for those daft reasons; it's pure unadulterated escapist fun. Nonsense, yes, but this is expensive nonsense of the highest order.

Waterworld isn't necessarily a bad film either. I just don't understand why it wasn't more popular on it's initial release. Perhaps it was always destined to fail? Back in 1994, the film's troubled and expensive Hawaiian shoot was much maligned by the press.

Hurricane damaged sets, reports of mass seasickness, and behind-the-scenes battles between its leading star and director (Kevin Costner and Kevin Reynolds) plagued production and made for perfect gossip column fodder (see a 1995 interview with Kevin Costner in *Entertainment Weekly*). [025]

The film's spiralling costs of $172m ($235m when including marketing and distribution) led it to being mocked and nicknamed *"Fishtar"* and *"Kevin's Gate"* – referring to two notorious big-budget flops, *Ishtar* (1987) and *Heaven's Gate* (1980). *Waterworld* was branded a lame duck long before its race had run!

When released in the summer of 1995, *Waterworld* tried, but failed, to escape the riptide of negative publicity set against it.

Even the Simpsons took a pop at the film's colossal budget.

Even *The Simpsons* took a pop at the film's colossal budget. In one cutaway-gag in the 1997 episode *The Springfield Files*, [026] the character Milhouse carefully deposits forty quarters (ten dollars) into a slot machine to play *Waterworld – The Game*.

Once loaded, he takes just one step forward before "Game over" flashes on the screen. The game then asks for a further forty quarters, to which Milhouse obliges!

The film has gone down in legend as one of the biggest box office bombs of the 20th century. However, this isn't technically true.

According to *Forbes* magazine in 2020, [027] despite only making $264m at the global box office, the film has slowly recouped its outgoings over the years through home entertainment and television distribution sales.

Time has also been relatively kind to *Waterworld*. The film has gained cult status with global audiences and spun-off a successful and highly praised stunt show, *Waterworld: A Live Sea War Spectacular*.

You can't argue the fact that all of the *Waterworld's* money is literally on-screen and then some!

The show features in several Universal Theme Parks, including Universal Studios Hollywood, where it has been successfully running for the last twenty-five years! Not bad going for an attraction based on a supposed mega-flop.

Decades after the wake of its box-office drama, *Waterworld* can be appreciated for being an epic visual feast and at no expense, too! Whereas most modern films would just key in their actors against a green screen, there's something admirable, yet absolutely insane, about the majority of *Waterworld* being filmed on the open ocean for real.

Crammed full of amazing sets, detailed costumes, epic stunts and huge explosions. *Waterworld's* money is showcased on-screen and then some! Everything is clearly pinned to the highest mast for all to see.

While managing to stay afloat financially, when viewed today some parts of *Waterworld* will make you want to submerge your head in embarrassment.

The film's treatment of women especially remains cringeworthy at best. In one scene, the film's leading female character (Helen) is whacked unconscious on the head with an oar by the film's supposed hero (the Mariner) (00:45:00).

In another scene, in a fit of rage, the same character picks up a small girl (Enola) and tosses her overboard into the ocean (00:51:17) for "talking too much".

Despite all this being part of Kevin Costner's Mariner character arc, these scenes make for uncomfortable viewing. The tinge of misogyny adds a level of murkiness to the film's waters. Extra-large pinches of sea salt are required when re-watching *Waterworld*; this was the '90s after all.

Even with this negativity, the film makes up for these errors with its environmental credentials. Perhaps *Waterworld's* most significant achievement lies in raising awareness of climate change issues.

Back in the '90s, society's perception of environmental concerns had gradually shifted away from the hazy hippy culture of the '60s and '70s. Science and practical solutions, including mass recycling and awareness of the green-house effect, had moved leaps and bounds in the public's consciousness.

Waterworld tried to capitalise on these issues. Looking back, it was probably the first of its kind, an "eco-blockbuster", raising awareness of climate change seductively concealed behind the façade of an explosive '90s action film.

'Live and let dry' - an inspired piece of Smoker propaganda.

In the years since, Roland Emmerich's disaster epic, *The Day after Tomorrow* (2004) **(pages 103–112)** was the next noble, if ham-fisted, attempt at picking up the environmental baton.

More factual or, dare I say, snobbier highbrow climate change documentaries followed from the likes of Al Gore with the Oscar-winning *An Inconvenient Truth* (2006) and Leonardo DiCaprio's *Before the Flood* (2016). Whilst these were raved about by critics, you've got to admit that nothing has captured the public's imagination quite like *Waterworld*.

This noble, if slightly flawed, blockbuster has probably been more successful in getting its environmental message across to a broader audience, much more than any niche documentary ever could.

I'm not saying that *Waterworld* is Greta Thunberg's favourite film, though part of me would secretly love it if it were. It's extremely doubtful though!

It's ironic that of all the disasters in this book, this is by far the most outlandish and crazy. Yet as hard as it is to believe, this is the one film where most of the events are destined to come true.

Bizarre as this may sound, we all know that the effects of climate change are happening now and will go on to affect life on this planet forever.

To what extent we don't know. It will ultimately depend on our actions today. The foundations of *Waterworld's* post-apocalyptic future might be considered soggy at best (more on this later).

And whilst we might not be scouring Rightmove just yet for convenient semi-detached properties halfway up Mount Snowdon, the film's underlying elements of truth give it an altogether disturbing and foreboding glimpse into the future.

Just add water

At the beginning of any historical drama or post-apocalyptic epic, you're presented with reams of text to read. You know the sort of thing: *"The year is…"*, *"The world has changed…"* etc.

Known as 'inter-titles', these short paragraphs are designed to set up a film's premise and instantly take you straight into the story (as well as strain your eyes at the same time).

Without them, you'd be Googling kings and queens of England midway through the film or scratching your head wondering what on Earth is going on.

Arguably, the most famous of all inter-titles belong to the *Star Wars* films. These iconic text crawls immediately make it a whole lot easier to transition into life in a "galaxy far, far away."

It's not always traditional text that can set up a plot. Visual alternatives can be as effective. One method is the transformation of a film studio logo.

Graphically, this can instantly say everything about a film's premise without uttering a single line or paragraph.

It's very easy to describe the plot of *Waterworld* as just another *Mad Max* rip-off with extra added water, because that's essentially what it is!

Waterworld does this simply and effectively. At the start of the film, the Universal Studios logo appears in silence. Essentially, it's a CGI version of planet Earth with the name of the studio in front.

As the text fades, the camera moves forward and silently sweeps across North America. Slowly but surely any remaining areas of land gradually disappear as the planet slowly turns blue (00:00:20)

As the world is engulfed by rising sea levels, the last remaining islands slowly disappear. The camera hits a cloud bank, and renowned voiceover artist Hal Douglas remarks: *"The future... The polar ice caps have melted, covering the Earth with water. Those who survived have adapted to a new world."*

The clouds disappear to reveal the film's title, with nothing but ocean for as far as the eye can see.

This sequence instantly sets you up for what's in store, and its subtlety leaves a lasting impression.

As a kid, I'd often pause the sequence over and over to try to work out the fate of the UK. However, the curvature of the Earth and the angle of the camera always obscured it from view. 'Toffee pennies' and '*Grease 2*' remember; strange child!

Waterworld is set hundreds of years in the future, where the last of the Earth's islands and landmasses have disappeared underwater.

All that's left are perma-tanned lone survivors known as drifters, who sail the planet's oceans, scavenging and trading whatever they can to survive. This is a harsh world, where dirt is a commodity and paper is considered a luxury.

It's very easy to describe the plot of *Waterworld* as just another *Mad Max* rip- off with added water, because that's essentially what it is! In an interview with *Starlog* magazine in 1995,[028] the film's writer Peter Rader said that in the late '80s the film was originally written as a Roger Corman B-movie version of *Mad Max*.

With a meagre budget of $5m planned, the producers may well have ended up filming at the local swimming baths! That's $230m cheaper than the final released version cost.

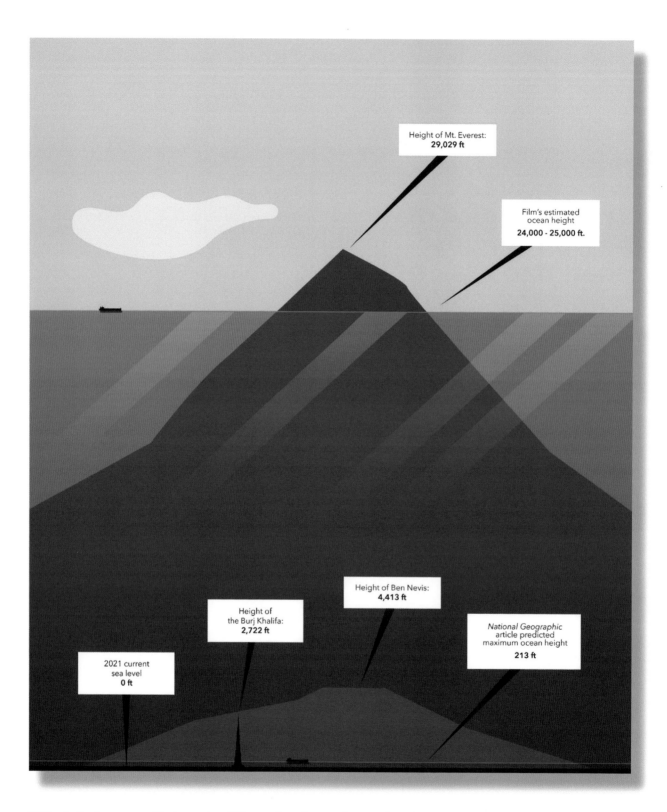

'Who left the tap on?' - how the different heights and water levels compare in the film and in real-life.

The parallels between *Mad Max* and the final version of the film run deep. *Waterworld* is about a brooding anti-hero, the Mariner (Kevin Costner), a lone drifter with a secret – he's a mutant with webbed feet and gills.

Instead of driving around the desert in a super-charged car like Max, the Mariner sails across the oceans in a gadget-laden Trimaran. And just like Mel Gibson's Max, the Mariner must reluctantly step forward and become the saviour of a small group of survivors, Helen (Jean Tripplehorn) and small child Enola (Tina Majorino).

Enola has a mysterious, cryptic map tattooed on her back, a map which apparently leads the way to the mythical dry land.

Stormy waters lie ahead, as in pursuit of Enola and her map are a warring group of marauders known as the Smokers.

Led by their tyrannical leader, the Deacon (Dennis Hopper), this band of modern-day pirates use jet-skis and motorboats to plunder and pillage the world around them. And they want that map!

The Smokers catch up to the Mariner, burn his boat and kidnap Enola (01:25:30). The Mariner swiftly sets out on a rescue mission to bring her back. He tracks down the Smokers to their floating lair, a rusty version of the infamous oil tanker, the Exxon Valdez (01:39:29).

He sneaks on-board and rescues Enola, but not before setting fire to the tanker's oil supply and blowing up the ship in the process (01:51:00)! The Deacon and the last remaining Smokers are defeated as the tanker sinks below the waves.

As the film draws to a close, the Mariner and several survivors, including Helen and Enola, find their way to dry land. Remarkably, this deserted tropical paradise 'in no way' looks like the Hawaiian islands (02:00:15).

It's only confirmed in deleted scenes of the 2020 Blu-ray that this island is the remains of the summit of Mount Everest. There's even an entire cut scene showing Helen and Enola stumbling across a plaque commemorating Tenzing and Hillary's ascension. It's hardly the most shocking of twists. Still, this confirmation raises more questions than answers about the fate of our extremely soggy planet.

Time & Tide

Waterworld means well with its environmental message, but its execution is massively flawed and full of holes. The first major flaw becomes apparent when comparing the premise against some actual science.

A 2013 article in *National Geographic* [029] stated that if all the polar ice caps melted, the oceans would only rise by 216 feet!

This rise in sea level would still be cataclysmic, with whole coastlines and countries wiped off the map. But unlike in *Waterworld*, it wouldn't lead to the disappearance of every single landmass.

In comparison, the height of Mount Everest is 29,029 feet, meaning there would be a shortfall of over 28,000 feet of water required to flood the planet.

Just where did all that extra water come from?! Did someone leave the tap on?

Just where did all that extra water come from?! Did someone leave the tap on?

Another flaw is the time it takes for the waters to rise. The *National Geographic* article also stated that scientists believe it could take up to 5,000 years for all the icecaps to melt, not the hundreds of years as indicated in the film. Or the thirty seconds it took for the planet to turn blue during the film's opening logo sequence.

That's not to say that we can all rest on our laurels and wait thousands of years for the literal floodgates to open.

A November 2019 article in *The Daily Mirror* [030] reported that within the next eighty years, the oceans could rise by 35 feet!

This sounds insignificant compared to the film's scenario, but on the contrary, it would be equally disastrous. UK cities like London, Liverpool and Hull would be heavily affected, whilst large areas of Lancashire, Lincolnshire and Cambridgeshire could also find themselves completely underwater.

Suppose we ignore all the scientific facts and go along with the premise that in 100 to 300 years, all the oceans will rise and flood every piece of land? In that case, *Waterworld's* plot falls down due to some good old-fashioned general knowledge.

Everyone knows that Mount Everest is the world's highest mountain. It's taught in geography lessons the world over from Doncaster to Dakar. It's such a commonly known fact it would probably be worth a measly £100 as a beginner's question on *Who Wants to Be a Millionaire?*

If the Earth's population continued to know this fact, then surely many people would have ventured to or tried to settle in the Himalayas during the hundreds of years that the ravages of climate change were taking place.

Now more questions arise for the fate of humanity. Could the human race have set up a new advanced technological society that could successfully cling to the cliffs of the mountain?

Certainly, newer cities like Dubai have emerged and grown in thirty years or less, so this could be a possibility. But, more likely, Mount Everest's well-known height would spark a range of issues for this last island on Earth.

With no other land to go to, survivors could face potential conflict, rising populations, famine, disease and food shortages.

Despite these questions, apart from small wooden huts and wild roaming horses, "Everest island" is left completely untouched and unpopulated in the film (02:01:10). Perhaps all those geography teachers conspired together to throw people off the scent and declare Mount Kilimanjaro as the highest mountain instead?!

If we tried to work out how the UK fared during the events of *Waterworld*, this would be a very short chapter indeed.

After all, the height difference between Ben Nevis* and the summit of Mount Everest** is 24,616 ft. That's nearly seven times the height of Britain's highest point. That's an awful lot of water to contend with **(see diagram, page 124).**

To work out the fate of the UK, we need to refer back to the earlier article from *National Geographic*, where the maximum predicted sea level increase would be 213 feet.

Comparing this to the film's 25,000 feet of water sounds insignificant, but it would still have dire consequences. Using topographic data from maps and *Floodmap.net* [031], we can work out what a future version of the UK might look like, and it's not looking good to be honest.

The country's coastlines, as we know and love them, would cease to exist. Every coastal town and city would be lost. Major cities like London, Liverpool, Manchester, Bristol, Edinburgh, Glasgow, Cardiff, Southampton, Norwich, Belfast, Newcastle and Dublin in the Irish Republic would all be submerged.

Networks of tiny islands would litter former areas of southeast England and the Irish mainland. Most of the UK mainland would be held together, but only just, by tiny outcrops and slithers of land.

There would be vast straits of water and new rivers to contend with too. Cambourne to Cumbernauld doesn't have the same ring to it as Land's End to John O'Groats.

There would also be very few cities or areas remaining high and dry. The smuggest and driest places would be reserved for central England, and the likes of Stoke-on-Trent, Coventry, Swindon, Wolverhampton, Bradford and Birmingham, with the latter in contention as the future capital of England.

Large swathes of mountainous areas in central Scotland and Wales would be the least affected by the rising waters. However, most Scottish and Welsh cities would be lost due to their coastal settings.

Despite the appeal of a "West Midlands archipelago", the only positive to this nightmare is it would take over 5,000 years to happen. This is the most extreme version of global warming and the worst it could possibly get.

Regardless of its faults, *Waterworld* provided a surprisingly realistic example of the future. We of course don't have to accept this fate, but the clock is ticking! If we all cooperate and work together, then hopefully, the plot of *Waterworld* will remain purely fictional – mullets, perma-tans, webbed feet and all!

*Ben Nevis 4,413 ft **Mt Everest 29,029 ft

Scenario

The following worst-case scenario is predicted from events in the film. As none of the following events were depicted on-screen, logic and rough estimations are applied throughout.

1 If the oceans rose by 213 feet, London would be one of the major casualties. Large swathes of the East of England would disappear under a large area of water stretching from Guildford in the south to Thatcham in the west, and Epping Forrest in the north.

2 Every coastal town and city in the UK and Ireland will cease to exist. Liverpool, Bristol, Edinburgh, Glasgow, Cardiff, Southampton, Belfast, Dublin, Newcastle, plus many more would be submerged.

3 The new coastline would submerge landlocked towns and cities, including Manchester, York, Norwich, Worcester, Derby, Oxford and Cambridge.

4 The Irish mainland would be split into smaller islands, surrounded by a new water inlet networks.

5 The UK mainland would be joined, only just! It would be connected by small slithers of land.

6 Mountainous regions of Wales and Scotland would be largely unaffected, however, many major Welsh and Scottish towns and cities would be wiped out due to their proximity to the coast.

7 Leeds, Sheffield, Nottingham, Wrexham and Motherwell will soon be unlikely new coastal towns and ports.

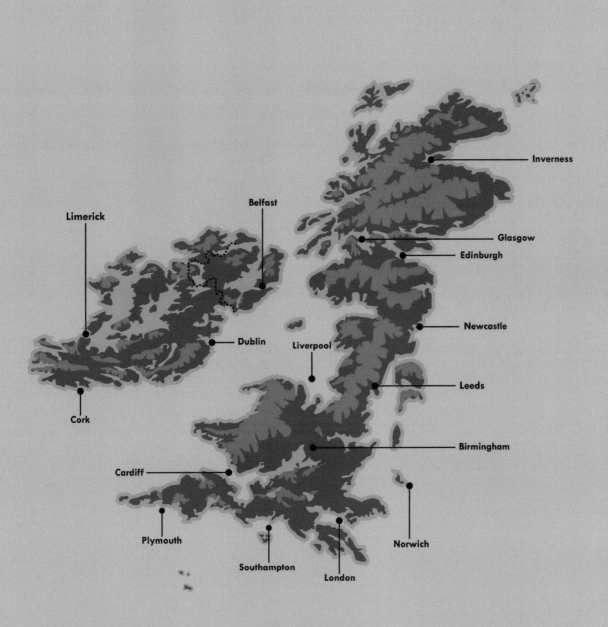

Inverness

Limerick

Belfast

Glasgow

Edinburgh

Newcastle

Dublin

Liverpool

Leeds

Cork

Birmingham

Cardiff

Plymouth

Norwich

Southampton

London

8 The driest areas would be reserved for Central England, including the new capital city of Birmingham. Other towns and cities sitting pretty would include Stoke-on-Trent, Coventry, Swindon, Wolverhampton and Bradford.

Survival outlook

Despite not being the total wash-out that *Waterworld's* dramatic license alluded to, this extreme version of global warming is nightmare fuel. There would be no community or area of the country safe from this dramatic change of landscape. Even my house in Northwich would become an oversized fish tank ornament.

Despite pondering what this brave new world might actually look like – lots of Scandinavian-style bridges or a twisted version of *'Miami Vice'* with lots of Brummy accents maybe? – I for one will definitely heed the warnings.

"My name is Max.
My world is fire and
blood" ₀₃₂

MAD MAX: FURY ROAD

(2015) Dir: George Miller

Behold the power of film! It can affect you tremendously without you realising. It can also mess with your emotions and make your sweat and tear ducts go haywire!

My most recent celluloid induced liquid experience' occurred within the men's toilets of Cheshire Oaks Vue Cinema.

No! It's probably not what you're thinking! For several minutes, I stood mesmerised and exhausted in front of the basin, looking back at my reflection in the mirror. I was a complete hot and sweaty mess!

After using almost an entire can of Sure women's deodorant from my friend's handbag, handed to me discreetly through the door, I can carefully say that I had never been through such an intense and exhilarating experience. *Mad Max: Fury Road* (2015), what had you done to me?!

Apart from the resulting small hole in the ozone layer created above Ellesmere Port that

day, the film was fantastic. *Mad Max: Fury Road* was a cinematic wild ride from beginning to end, with a thunderous pace that never slipped up. Unexpectedly, it stands up there as one of the best action films of the last decade, or – dare I say it? – of all time! Based on George Miller's iconic post-apocalyptic action series of the '70s and '80s, *Mad Max: Fury Road* had a massive cinematic legacy to live up to.

With a long and troubled production stretching nearly two decades, as the film put it, the road to "shiny and chrome" success at the "gates of Valhalla" was not guaranteed.

The first film was an independent Australian cinematic marvel. *Mad Max* (1979) starred a fresh-faced Mel Gibson in the title role, as a broken and unhinged ex-traffic cop who goes on a rampage of revenge after witnessing the death of his wife and child at the hands of a crazed motorcycle gang.

As the series developed, the budget increased, and the sequels became wilder and even more dystopian. *Mad Max 2: The Road Warrior* (1981) would go on to define post-apocalyptic cinema and be emulated for years to come **(see *Waterworld*, pages 117–130).**

In this sequel, Max takes on the Good, the Bad and the S&M leather-clad in a series of spectacular chase sequences featuring cars, tankers and a feral "dog boy" with a boomerang!

The third film, *Mad Max: Beyond the Thunderdome* (1985), was the point where the wheels began to come off. The only memorable piece in this instalment was that it starred Tina Turner and featured her karaoke classic *"We Don't Need Another Hero"*.

Mad Max: Fury Road aimed to re-introduce Max and his crazy post-apocalyptic world to a new generation of cinema-goers. It was a gamble at the time and had every conceivable obstacle going against it.

The first major stumbling block was time. It had been a whopping thirty years since the last film was released with a whimper at the box office. The usual sequel rule of thumb, wherein the longer the gap, the worse the film **(see *Independence Day: Resurgence*, pages 81–90)** could definitely be wagged in the direction of *Fury Road*.

In Max's three-decade absence, a lot had happened. Australian director George Miller had taken on the polar opposite worlds of talking pigs in *Babe: Pig in the City* (1998) and dancing penguins in *Happy Feet* (2006), while its leading star Mel Gibson had undergone a turbulent and much-publicised fall from grace after THAT infamous DUI arrest in 2006.

Since the early 2000s, Miller had made numerous troubled attempts to get *Mad Max: Fury Road* going again, with multiple production shutdowns across two continents. He was ready to begin production in Namibia way back in 2003. Speaking to *The New York Times* [033] in 2020, he remarked:

> *"But then 9/11 happened and everything changed. We couldn't get insured. We couldn't get our vehicles transported. It just collapsed."*

The marathon process led to the gradual removal of Gibson in favour of Tom Hardy in the Max role. After a long, difficult shoot, *Mad Max: Fury Road* was finally ready for release in May 2015. But after its long absence, would there still be a connection with its audience?

That summer was an extremely packed season at the cinema. Big releases including the likes of *Avengers: The Age of Ultron* (2015), *Minions* (2015) and *Fast & Furious 7* (2015) were competing at the box office. And the title of biggest film of the summer was reserved for the money-printing juggernaut, *Jurassic World* (2015)!

Despite all the competition, *Fury Road* proved everyone wrong. As one of the few Rated 15 releases that summer, the film stood out in all its gritty crazed glory and offered cinema-goers a totally different, exhilarating and far from safe alternative.

With global box office takings of $375.4m, the film brutally tore off the sequel rule of thumb, rolled down the window and tossed it into the dusty desert road behind!

Always *Aqua-Cola*

Fury Road takes place in the not-too-distant future, several years after the events of the previous film. However all that's carried across are Max Rockatansky (Tom Hardy) and his GT Falcon muscle car. Everything else is turned on its head and completely new!

After the ravages of nuclear war, famine and drought have brought society to its knees, any survivors in this harsh world are forced to cling to life in settlements scattered across a never-ending desert. Only the brutal and brave endure in this radioactive landscape known as the Wasteland.

Those in power rule with an iron fist and control the four necessities that keep this future society running. (And no, Wi-Fi is not on the list!) These include: water (known as *Aqua-Cola*), munitions, fuel and eh…erm…. breast milk, otherwise known as *Mother's Milk*. The settlements operate as cartels and trade back and forth with one another in this warped economy. They also rally and work together to keep one another in power.

They're basically twisted versions of the farmers Boggis, Bunce and Bean from Roald Dahl's classic children's book *The Fantastic Mr Fox*, except with added breast pumps and bullet medallions! The formidable Immortan Joe (Hugh Keays-Byrne) more or less runs the show from high above the Citadel, a desert outcrop with an infinite supply of *Aqua-Cola*.

This is pumped up from an underground source to the top of the rock formation, which bears a lush paradise of crops and plant-life (00:05:20). This is a tale of two Citadels. On the ground level are Joe's loyal subjects, hordes of malnourished and desperate people who live in dustbowl conditions.

All day, they clamber around with pots and pans, waiting on Joe's every whim to sparingly release bursts of water from pipes high above the cliff face.

"Do not, my friends, become addicted to water. It will take hold of you, and you will resent its absence!" declares Joe via a megaphone to the masses below (00:08:38).

As well as monopolising the elements, Joe single-handedly and creepily controls the birth population too. Put it this way: we know who'll be getting all of the cards on Father's Day!

All the boys are raised as warriors, known as War Boys. They protect the Citadel in an assortment of customised vehicles and perform Joe's dirty work, including hunting, kidnapping and defending transports. Also known as Half-lives, these War Boys are unfortunately plagued with sickness from radiation poisoning and regularly require blood transfusions to prolong their lives (00:11:09).

The girls however have the worst of it! The prettiest ones are destined to become part of Joe's beloved prize breeding stock, known as the First Wives, who make way for future generations.

Any girls who fail to meet Joe's beauty requirements are set to become part of the Milking Room, providing all the Citadel's protein needs via a never-ending supply of breast milk (00:12:45). Away from the Citadel,

'Obey or else! ' - a propaganda-inspired 'Immortan Joe' poster.

Oil Wars, followed by Water Wars, topped with the cherry of a thermonuclear fallout.

further down Fury Road, are other settlements that complete this rather twisted economy.

Supplying all your munitions needs is the gun-toting War Lord known as the Bullet Farmer (Richard Carter) (00:52:50), whilst the People Eater (John Howard) monopolises all the Wasteland's gasoline production from a former oil refinery known as Gas Town (00:43:35).

Fury Road is ultimately an end of the line film, where mankind is taken to the precipice and the absolute limits of lawlessness and desperation. Ironic that mankind's hero and saviour is not a man at all!

The film truly belongs to Charlize Theron's warrior trucker, Imperator Furiosa. Tom Hardy's Max is simply along for the ride, as we the audience cling on to his sweaty back and hang on for dear life.

The plot follows Furiosa as she goes rogue from Immortan Joe and tries to smuggle several of his prize breeding wives to freedom, hidden inside the back of her tanker. Their aim is to get to the Green Place, a near-mythical land which promises an endless supply of plants and vegetation.

Enraged, Immortan Joe gets wind of her plan and dispatches his armada of vehicles and War Boys in hot pursuit! He also rallies the neighbouring clans from Gas Town and the Bullet Farm to assist. Max soon gets swept into the chaos in some of the greatest chase sequences of all time! Cars, motorbikes, tankers, HGVs, tanks, monster trucks! Everything is thrown on-screen in glorious carnage!

Eventually, Max sides with Furiosa. But their dreams of finding the fabled Green Place are shattered after it's revealed the land has become toxic and succumbed to pollution (01:20:30). With nowhere else to go, Max and Furiosa hatch a plan to go back the way they came and claim back the (now defenceless) Citadel, taking on Joe and the clans once and for all!

The film is the equivalent of one of those freefall rollercoasters that propels you 100mph across a horizontal track to a sudden 90-degree vertical assent.

But what goes up must come down; as the ride plummets backwards, the plot returns in the same direction it came. Cue more screaming, carnage and exhilarating action on the way back down. By the time you exit the thrill ride and Max and Furiosa defeat Joe and take the Citadel (01:49:20), you too, like me in that Cheshire Oaks toilet, will be in serious need of an extra-long deodorant top-up! 24-hour protection? Who are they kidding?!

Anarchy in the UK

As the film takes place in a post-apocalyptic Australia, there's no definitive answer to what happens elsewhere, especially in the UK. The fate of the world is never mentioned. To work out what a potential future might look like, we have to make some basic predictions from events in the film.

The first indication of any global events occurs during the film's opening title sequence. This features short soundbites set against some footage of nuclear blasts. Random voices utter the words:

> "Oil wars", "We are killing for guzzoline!", "The world is actually running out of water", "Now there's the Water Wars", "Thermonuclear skirmish", "The Earth is sour!", "Our bones are poisoned", "We have become half-life" (00:00:20).

Oil Wars, followed by Water Wars, topped by the cherry of thermonuclear fallout. This sounds like an extremely grim version of the future.

As Europe or other parts of the world aren't mentioned, there's no knowing if this sequence of events would apply here, especially in the UK. It would be extremely doubtful that this side of the world would completely escape the incoming nuclear apocalypse, however.

The UK, of course, has an entirely different ecology from Australia, so we don't know if the oceans here would disappear and become endless desert. Other possibilities include surrounding seas turning toxic or acidic and made completely inaccessible.

A post-apocalyptic UK under the same template as Mad Max: Fury Road might be difficult to predict. Who knows, instead of souped-up muscle cars and monster trucks, we could have double- decker buses with additional flame throwers or Mondeos and Yaris's with metal spikes!

The power structure of the UK would probably be turned on its head. After years of nuclear war, governments could be eradicated, and critical infrastructures, including financial, commercial and communications, would no longer be significant in this hostile new world.

The only thing we can focus on to indicate the fate of the UK is to apply Fury Road's four necessities of Aqua-Cola, Fuel, Munitions and erh...Mother's Milk. These new dependencies would consume the UK and cause a potential mass migration shift.

Any survivors would abandon the desolated cities and move to previously insignificant areas of the country. Places like Harrogate, Buxton, Bath and the Ochil Hills of Scotland have the potential to become the new Citadels due to their abundance of underground spring water. [034]

The North Sea oil fields, the south of England and parts of Lancashire, known for their controversial shale gas production sites, would be likely contenders for potential Gas Towns. Any remaining military bases, ports, or firing ranges like Portsmouth, Rosyth or the Bulford Camp on Salisbury Plain would have the potential to become the UK's Bullet Farms.

The less said about potential Mother's Milk suppliers, the better! Who knows, there could be armour-plated milk tankers and milk floats with additional metal spikes? In this world, nothing would surprise me!

Scenario

The following worst-case scenario is predicted from events in the film. As none of the following events were depicted on-screen, logic and rough estimations are applied throughout.

1 After many years of battles for oil and water and the effects of Nuclear fallout, the UK would be decimated. Much of the land would be poisoned and uninhabitable. The oceans and surrounding seas would have either have been evaporated into desert or reduced to toxic waste ground.

2 Anyone living in cities or urban environments will have eventually fled to new settlements across the country.

3 Areas known for their spring water production would become the UK's next Citadels. Places like Buxton, Bath, Harrogate and the Ochil Hill hills of Scotland would be the likeliest contenders.

4 Areas in the south of England and Lancashire, known for their shale gas production, could become the UK's primary energy power resources in this post-apocalyptic world.

5 The North Sea oil fields would become vitally important and provide the lion's share of fuel for vehicles and settlements in the UK.

6 Any remaining military bases, ports or firing ranges would become the UK's likeliest Bullet farms. Places like Portsmouth, Rosyth or the Bulford Camp on the Salisbury Plain would be contenders.

Limerick

Belfast

Inverness

The Ochil Hills

Edinburgh

Cork

Dublin

Newcastle

Liverpool

Harogate

Buxton

Cardiff

Southampton

London

Survival outlook

It's a tough call, but the best chance for surviving this nightmarish landscape is to get in on the action of one of the settlements and keep your head down.

Don't bother with the Bullet Towns or Gas Towns – they'd be far too dirty. Instead, stick with the Citadels and go to the likes of Harrogate, Buxton or Bath, where you'll have all the water supplies you need.

Overall, if you can make it through the Oil Wars, Water Wars, nuclear fallout, and poisoned Earth, then avoid all craziness from fellow human beings, who might want to rob you, kill you, eat you, or skin you alive and wear you as a new coat then.... actually you're doing rather well!

SURVIVAL MATRIX

That's it! It's all over! Your safe to come out now!

The council's been round and quickly managed to sweep the streets of all the rubble. All the remaining emaciated zombies and discarded alien tentacles will be removed in the morning. Just don't expect anything to be done about those potholes anytime soon!

As the all-clear sirens fall silent, you can finally venture out of your panic rooms, basements, attics and step out into the sun. So how did you get on? Were you able to survive each cataclysm in this book? Or was it a case of "game over" in every chapter?

To see how your nearest town or city compares against one another, I've created this unique Survival matrix.

Every British and Irish location mentioned in this book drawn up in a long list. Each location has then been marked against all 10 featured films and given a predicted survival score.

The scoring is as follows:

5 = Guaranteed survival
4 = A better chance of survival
3 = Mixed chances
2 = Low chance survival
1 = No chance of survival

The maximum accumulated score for each location is 50 points. The higher the combined score, the safer your location. The lower the score, then I'd probably consider contacting your estate agent.

	GoldenEye	28 Days Later	Kingsman: The Secret Service	Independence Day	Wat of the Worlds	Independence Day: Resurgence	Deep Impact	The Day After Tomorrow	Waterworld	Mad Max: Fury Road	Total
Aberdeen	4	4	2	5	1	3	5	2	1	3	*30*
Bath	4	2	1	5	2	3	2	2	1	4	26
Balmoral	4	4	3	1	1	3	5	2	4	1	28
Belfast	4	5	1	2	1	3	1	2	1	1	21
Birmingham	4	1	1	1	1	3	2	2	4	1	20
Bournemouth	4	2	1	4	1	3	1	2	1	1	20
Bradford	4	2	1	4	2	3	4	2	5	1	28
Brighton	3	1	1	2	1	3	1	2	1	1	16
Bristol	4	1	1	3	1	3	1	2	1	1	17
Buxton	4	3	2	5	2	3	5	2	4	1	*31*
Cambourne	4	2	1	5	1	3	5	2	1	1	25
Cambridge	3	1	1	4	1	3	2	2	4	1	22
Cardiff	4	1	1	4	1	1	1	2	1	1	17
Channel Islands, The	4	5	3	5	2	3	1	2	1	1	25
Chester	4	1	1	3	1	3	2	2	1	1	19
Chequers	4	2	1	1	1	3	1	2	1	1	17
Cleethorpes	4	2	1	5	2	3	5	2	1	1	26
Coventry	4	1	1	2	1	3	2	2	5	1	22
Crawley	2	1	1	1	1	3	1	2	1	1	*14*
Cumbernauld	4	2	1	5	2	3	5	2	4	1	29
Derby	4	2	1	5	1	3	2	2	1	1	22
Derry / Londonderry	4	5	1	5	1	3	1	2	1	1	24
Doncaster	4	2	1	5	1	3	5	2	1	1	25
Edinburgh	4	2	1	4	1	3	5	2	1	1	24
Ellesmere Port	4	2	1	3	2	3	2	2	1	1	23
Epping Forrest	1	2	3	1	3	3	1	2	1	1	18
Exeter	4	3	1	5	2	1	1	2	1	1	21
Glasgow	4	2	1	4	1	3	4	2	2	1	24
Glastonbury	4	3	1	5	3	3	1	2	1	1	24
Gloucester	4	2	1	5	1	2	1	2	1	1	20
Guildford	1	1	1	2	1	3	1	2	1	1	*14*
Harrogate	4	3	1	5	1	3	5	2	3	4	*31*
Inverness	4	4	2	5	2	3	5	2	1	1	*29*
Isle of Man, The	4	5	2	5	3	3	3	2	1	1	*29*
Isle of Wight, The	3	5	2	5	3	3	1	2	1	1	26
John O' Groats	4	4	4	5	3	3	5	2	4	1	*36*
Lake District, The	4	4	4	5	3	3	5	2	3	1	*34*
Land's End	4	4	4	5	3	1	1	2	2	1	27
Leeds	4	1	1	4	1	3	4	2	4	1	25
Leicester	4	1	1	4	1	3	1	2	1	1	19
Liverpool	4	1	1	1	1	3	2	2	1	1	17

	GoldenEye	28 Days Later	Kingsman: The Secret Service	Independence Day	Wat of the Worlds	Independence Day: Resurgence	Deep Impact	The Day After Tomorrow	Waterworld	Mad Max: Fury Road	Total
London	1	1	1	1	1	3	1	2	1	1	*13*
Luton	1	1	1	1	1	3	1	2	1	1	*13*
Maidenhead	2	1	1	1	1	3	1	2	1	1	*14*
Manchester	4	1	1	1	1	3	2	2	1	1	17
Middlesbrough	4	2	1	5	1	3	5	2	1	1	25
Motherwell	4	2	1	5	1	3	5	2	4	1	28
Mt. Ben Nevis	4	5	5	5	4	3	5	2	5	1	*39*
Mt. Snowden	4	4	5	5	4	3	5	2	5	1	*38*
Newcastle	4	2	1	5	1	3	5	2	2	1	26
Northwich	4	3	3	4	2	3	2	2	1	1	23
Norwich	3	2	2	5	1	3	2	2	1	1	22
Nottingham	4	2	1	2	1	3	2	2	4	1	22
Ochil Hills, The	4	4	4	5	3	3	5	2	5	4	*39*
Oxford	4	3	1	2	1	3	1	2	1	1	19
Portsmouth	4	3	1	1	1	3	1	2	1	4	19
Plymouth	4	3	1	1	1	1	1	2	1	1	16
Reading	4	2	1	2	1	3	1	2	1	1	18
Rosyth	4	4	1	1	1	3	5	2	1	3	25
Sandringham	4	3	2	1	1	3	1	2	1	1	19
Sheffield	4	2	1	2	1	3	3	2	4	1	23
Shetlands, The	4	4	1	5	3	3	4	2	2	1	29
Slough	2	1	1	2	1	3	1	2	1	1	15
Southend on sea	1	3	1	2	1	3	1	2	1	1	*14*
Southampton	3	2	1	2	1	1	1	2	1	1	*13*
Stevenage	2	3	1	1	1	3	1	2	1	1	*14*
Stoke-on-Trent	4	2	1	2	1	3	2	2	5	1	23
Swindon	4	2	1	4	1	3	1	2	5	1	24
Swansea	4	2	1	5	1	1	1	2	1	1	19
Thatcham	4	2	1	2	1	3	1	2	1	1	18
Torquay	4	3	2	5	2	1	1	2	1	1	22
Woking	4	3	1	1	1	3	1	2	1	1	16
Wolverhampton	4	2	1	2	1	3	1	2	5	1	22
Worcester	4	2	1	5	1	3	1	2	1	1	21
Wrexham	4	3	2	5	2	3	2	2	4	1	28
York	4	2	1	5	1	3	4	2	1	1	24
Cork	4	5	2	5	1	1	1	2	2	1	24
Dublin	4	5	1	3	1	3	1	2	2	1	23
Galway	4	5	2	5	2	1	1	2	1	1	24
Limerick	4	5	2	5	1	1	1	2	1	1	23

Results

From the results of the Survival matrix, the following locations would come out on top with the most points:

39	The Ochil Hills
36	John O' Groats
34	The Lake District
31	Buxton
31	Harrogate
30	Aberdeen
29	Inverness
29	Isle of Man

The common themes include:

- **Head north** – The further north you go, the safer you'll be.

- **Stay remote** – Try to avoid any populated areas. Stay as in-hospitable as you can!

- **Bring a bottle** – Head to areas known for their spring water resources

On the flipside, the locations with the lowest survival ratings would be:

13	London
13	Luton
13	Southampton
14	Crawley
14	Guildford
14	Maidenhead
14	Southend on sea
14	Stevenage

The common themes here include:

- **Capital punishment** – London and all of the southeast of England would take on the brunt of kicking in each film.

- **Avoid the south coast**– Avoid the South coast of England at all costs. Alien attacks, tsunamis and rising sea levels will make this area a magnet for apocalyptic destruction.

BIBLIOGRAPHY

001 "GoldenEye" (1995)
Director: Martin Campbell
© 1995 Danjaq Inc. and United Artists Pictures Inc.

002 The Sun
"WARNING SIGNS Pentagon developing ways to detect electromagnetic pulses to prevent 'Pearl Harbour-style' surprise nuclear EMP attack"
Samantha Lock, Jul 18 2020

https://www.thesun.co.uk/news/us-news/12162589/pentagon-detecting-electromagnetic-pearl-harbor-surprise-attack/

003 Forbes magazine
"China Has 'First-Strike' Capability To Melt U.S. Power Grid With Electromagnetic Pulse Weapon",
James Konca, Jun 25, 2020

https://www.forbes.com/sites/jamesconca/2020/06/25/china-develops-first-strike-capability-with-electromagnetic-pulse/

004 "28 Days Later" (2002)
Director: Danny Boyle
© 2002, Fox Searchlight

005 Filmmaker magazine
"The Deceased World", Kim Newman, 2003

https://filmmakermagazine.com/archives/issues/summer2003/features/diseased_world.php

006 "The Kingsman: The Secret Service" (2015)
Director: Matthew Vaughn
© 2015, 20th Century Fox

007 Cheshire-live.co.uk
"007 fans to stage Chester protest against "boring" Bond movie", Oct 30 2008

https://www.cheshire-live.co.uk/news/chester-cheshire-news/007-fans-stage-chester-protest-5232750.amp

008 Entertainment Weekly
"From the archives: Roger Moore reflects on his James Bond legacy", Chris Nashawaty, May 23, 2017

https://ew.com/movies/2008/12/09/roger-moore-best-james-bond/

009   Gizmodo.com
"Matthew Vaughn Explains The Problem With Modern-Day Spy Movies", Meredith Woerner, Feb 12 2015

https://gizmodo.com/matthew-vaughn-explains-the-problem-with-modern-day-spy-1685436781

010   Global Data Systems
"Cellular vs. Satellite: Understanding the Differences"

https://www.getgds.com/resources/blog/connectivity/cellular-vs-satellite-understanding-the-differences

011   Stelladoradus.com
https://www.stelladoradus.com/mobile-coverage-area-check-buy/

012   "Independence Day" (1996)
Director: Roland Emmerich
©1996, 20th Century Fox

013   "The Simpsons"
Episode: "Summer of 4 Ft. 2"
Season 7 // Episode 25
Directed by Mark Kirkland
Written by Dan Greaney
May 19 1996
©1996, 20th Century Fox

014   UK population data
https://www.citypopulation.de/en/uk/cities/ua/

015   Independence Day Wiki
https://independenceday.fandom.com/wiki/War_of_1996

016   "War of the Worlds" (2005)
Director: Steven Spielberg
©2005, Paramount / DreamWorks

017   "Independence Day: Resurgence" (2016)
Director: Roland Emmerich
©2016, 20th Century Fox

018   Yahoo News
"Director Roland Emmerich regrets making 'Independence Day: Resurgence'", Hannah Flint, 06 Nov 2019

https://uk.news.yahoo.com/news/independence-day-director-roland-emmerich-regrets-making-sequel-170655100.html?guce_referrer=aHR0cHM6Ly93d3cuZ29vZ2xlLmNvbV7Lw&guce_referrer_sig=AQAAAM3JjYoCL2mwJZCn4ZYtO5_VzebhHxDuPMqqY4aA8mSRutaQoGeihMAP900fsn5cRXpliAhZ1IUi1iG0dzMav_h-6A1E_0evwdsq-Iq6pzdXgAvPTM_5Yxuzn6q7Xnr0QbYoLOSOASJ4_cXhtEPaBW47ajRasHm9VFr1TTcg2ehx&guccounter=1

019   "Deep Impact" (1998)
Director: Mimi Leder
©1996, Paramount / DreamWorks

020   The Guardian
"A last wave goodbye", Duncan Steel, 11 Apr 2002

https://www.theguardian.com/science/2002/apr/11/physicalsciences.research

021   "The Day after Tomorrow" (2004)
Director: Roland Emmerich
©2004, 20th Century Fox

022   Collider.com
"Roland Emmerich Talks 'Midway', His Lowkey Politics & Being Known as the "Master of Disaster", Helen Barlow, 09 Oct 2019

https://collider.com/roland-emmerich-interview-midway-career/

023   Businessinsider.com
"The film 'The Day After Tomorrow' foretold a real and troubling trend: The ocean's water-circulation system is weakening", Aylin Woodward, Mar 25, 2019

https://www.businessinsider.com/day-after-tomorrow-was-right-and-wrong-about-climate-shifts-2019-3?r=US&IR=

024   "Waterworld" (1995)
Director: Kevin Reynolds
©1995, Universal Pictures

025   Entertainment Weekly
"Dangerous when wet: Inside the tumultuous times of Waterworld", Jess Cagle, 01 Mar 2009

https://ew.com/article/2009/03/01/waterworlds-tumultuous-times-ew-archive/

026   "The Simpsons"
Episode: "The Springfield Files"
Season 8 // Episode 10
Directed by Steven Dean Moore
Written by Reid Harrison
Jan 12, 1997
©1997, 20th Century Fox

027   Forbes magazine
"Kevin Costner's 'Waterworld' Was The Biggest Box Office Bomb That Wasn't", Scott Mendelson, 28 July 2020

https://www.forbes.com/sites/scottmendelson/2020/07/28/waterworld-starring-kevin-costner-was-the-biggest-box-office-bomb-that-wasnt/?sh=1915bbc2607d

028   Starlog Magazine
"Rime of the future Mariner", Kim Howard Johnson, Sep 2005

https://archive.org/details/starlog_magazine-218/page/n83/mode/2up?view=theater

029   National Geographic Magazine
https://www.nationalgeographic.com/magazine/article/rising-seas-ice-melt-new-shoreline-maps

030   The Daily Mirror
"Chilling 'Doomsday map' shows how UK will be left underwater in 80 years' time", Neil Murphy, 3 Nov 2019

https://www.mirror.co.uk/news/uk-news/chilling-doomsday-map-shows-how-20803818

031   Floodmap
https://www.floodmap.net

032   "Mad Max: Fury Road" (2015)
Director: George Miller
©2016, Warner Bros

033   New York Times
"Mad Max: Fury Road -An Oral History of a modern Classic", Kyle Buchanan, 12 May 2020

https://www.nytimes.com/2020/05/12/movies/mad-max-fury-road-oral-history.html

034   Keele University
"How Brexit could drain Britain's bottled mineral water industry dry", Alexandre Nobajas , 21 Feb 2018

https://www.keele.ac.uk/discover/news/2018/february/

INDEX

THANK YOU

I want to personally thank Mum, Dad, Andrea and all my family and friends for all their love and support over the last few months, especially during lockdown.

I'd also personally like to thank my besties Lew, Becca and Libby for all their encouragement. Now this book's complete I can finally put my feet up and get Amazon Prime!

A special thanks also goes out to; Tom Feltham, Jas Rao, Stuart Fleming and my ex-Specsavers alumni; including Charlotte Richfield, Sam Jessop and Heather 'Queen of the Zombies' McClinton, for all their help in deciphering my ramblings and making it all make grammatical sense.

I'd also like to personally thank you, the reader, for taking a chance on my book and for coming along the journey with me, as a first-time author.

TOM J BARROW

Tom was born in Merseyside, England in 1982. He grew-up in his hometown of Northwich, Cheshire where he still resides.

Tom graduated with a BA (Hons) in Design and Art Direction from Manchester Metropolitan University.

His passion for film holds no bounds. In his early twenties Tom worked for Blockbuster Video (he still owns his card and name badge!). He later worked as a voluntary film critic for his local newspaper.

Tom works full time as a Digital Learning Designer.

Absolute Disaster is Tom's debut book.

Printed in Great Britain
by Amazon